TOM SMITH performed with several cult bands in the 1980s and after some years as a manager for independent record labels became a freelance writer on musical subjects. He has written biographies on Blondie and the Ramones and is author of a BBC radio drama on the relationship between Harry Houdini and Sir Arthur Conan Doyle. His artwork has appeared on posters and record covers and his 2011 exhibition 'Jockey Full of Bourbon' centred on paintings of Frank Sinatra, Elvis Presley and Tom Waits.

One for My Baby

A SINATRA COCKTAIL COMPANION

TOM SMITH

PETER OWEN

PETER OWEN PUBLISHERS
81 Ridge Road, London N8 9NP

Peter Owen books are distributed in the USA and Canada by
Independent Publishers Group/Trafalgar Square
814 North Franklin Street, Chicago, IL 60610, USA

First published in Great Britain 2015 by Peter Owen Publishers

Cased ISBN 978-0-7206-2016-0
Epub ISBN 978-0-7206-2017-7
Mobipocket ISBN 978-0-7206-2018-4
PDF ISBN 978-0-7206-2019-1

A catalogue record for this book is available from the British Library.

Designed by Danica Rosso

Printed by Printworks Global Ltd, London and Hong Kong

To Helen
All my love
All of it
Always

Preface

T his is a book that happily combines two of my abiding personal interests – the music of Frank Sinatra and fancy drinks. These are two subjects that could be considered as concomitant. *One for My Baby* is a biography of Sinatra, but it is one that concentrates on a particular feature of his life – his abiding relationship with alcohol. Of course, considering his life and times through his drinking is a conceit, but it is hardly the most fanciful of conceits. There are more than enough stories, anecdotes, myths, legends and facts to make a compelling case that his drinking was an integral part of his character, his lifestyle and, by extension, his creative output. His two most enduring personas – Rat Pack leader and solitary small-hours drinker – might seem diametrically opposed (the Chairman of the Board and the loser) but were united by the glasses in their hands. Alcohol was a constant throughout his life, and his devotion to drink outlasted any love affair. Only the music was more important.

Sinatra undoubtedly lived the lush life, and Billy Strayhorn's skewed ballad on the subject could have been a much more fitting personal theme tune than 'My Way'. Sinatra attempted 'Lush Life' during the recording of *Only the Lonely* but abandoned the notoriously difficult song after several attempts, telling his piano player Bill Miller that he had decided to leave that one for Nat King Cole.

This book, then, traces some of that lush life and aims to give a flavour of it by detailing some of his personal drinking lore and outlining some of the traditions he followed or inspired. There are also accounts of some of his favourite watering holes – from legendary saloons such as Toots Shor's and Jilly's to celebrity nightclubs like El Morocco and the

Stork Club – and profiles of famous drinking buddies, including Bogart, Dean and Sammy.

As well as informing the reader of where he drank and who he drank with, this book functions as a practical cocktail manual with instructions on how to construct, present and consume some of the fancy drinks Sinatra and companions were known to have enjoyed, from classic bourbon cocktails such as the Old Fashioned through to Smoked Martinis as well several favoured curatives for the inevitable alcoholic remorse, including Sinatra's own ultimate hangover cure the Ramos Gin Fizz.

All of this knowledge may not grant you Frank-like status, but, late at night with a glass in your hand and one of his records playing, it might just feel like it.

Notes on the recipes and the drinks

In all of the recipes in this book a measure is equivalent to the larger cup on a standard American double jigger, that is, 1 US fluid oz. For more on this see 'Some Notes on the Particulars'.

Whiskey/whisky: unless stated otherwise (Irish whiskey, for example) for the purposes of this book whiskey means bourbon, rye or Tennessee varieties; whisky from Scotland is referred to throughout as Scotch.

Vermouths: these have either a red- or white-wine base. The general rule is that red vermouth is sweet (and used for drinks such as the Manhattan) while white vermouth is by and large dry (although there are some popular sweet whites) and is used for Martinis.

Contents

8 | Preface

13 | The Last Saloon Singer

33 | Some Notes on the Particulars
Measure for Measure
Bar Exam
Some Toasts: Traditional Sinatra Salutes

41 | Jack Daniel's Original Test Pilot
How Sinatra Took His
Classic Bourbon Cocktails: *Manhattan, Old Fashioned, Whiskey Sour, Ward 8, Algonquin Cocktail, Whiskey Sour in the Rough, Bob Hope's Rye Lemonade, Benny Goodman's Admiral Cocktail*

54 | Watering Holes: Toots Shor's – *Vodka Gimlet*
58 | Drinking Buddies: Joe E. Lewis

61 | 'Tini Time
A Potted History of the Martini: *Dry Martini, Flame of Love Martini, The Vesper, Layaway, Gibson (1), Gibson (2), Vodkatini*
74 | Watering Holes: P.J. Clarke's – *Sidecar*
76 | Drinking Buddies: Humphrey Bogart

79 | Exotic Booze
For When You Could Use Some: *Mai Tai, Daiquiri, Floridita Special, Mojito, Cuba Libre, Blue Hawaii, Margarita, Caipirinha, Bossa Nova, Negroni*

90 | Watering Holes: Villa Capri – *Americano*
93 | Drinking Buddies: Mike Romanoff

99 | Alcoholic Remorse
Curatives for the Inevitable: *Ramos Gin Fizz, Bloody Mary, Death in the Afternoon, Zombie, Corpse Reviver, Stinger, Red Devil, Prairie Oyster*

106 | Watering Holes: Jilly's – *Boilermaker*
109 | Drinking Buddies: Jimmy Van Heusen

113 | High Society
Upmarket Watering Holes: 21 Club – *South Side*; Chasen's – *Chasen's Banana Punch*; Pump Room – *Bath Cure, Sherry Flip*; El Matador – *Blood and Sand, Matador*; Chi Chi – *Chi Chi Cocktail*; Ciro's – *After Dinner Special, Vesuvius*; Stork Club – *Julius Special, Stork Club Cooler, Stork Club Cocktail*; El Morocco – *El Morocco*; Copacabana – *Copacabana Cocktail* French Champagne: *Black Velvet, Mimosa, Lee Miller's Frobisher, Champagne Cocktail*

141 | How Did All These People Get in My Room?
The Rat Pack: Dino – *Scotch Rocks*; Sammy – *Salty Dog*; Peter – *Bellini*; Joey – *Roy Rogers*

173 | Watering Holes: The Sands – *Atomic Cocktail*

177 | Last Word: Rat-Pack Patter from Frank and Dean

179 | Further Reading
181 | Select Discography
187 | Index of Cocktail Recipes by Chief Ingredient
189 | Index of Watering Holes
189 | Acknowledgements

11

'Still a belter, baby!' Sinatra on stage in 1970

The Last Saloon Singer

Francis Albert Sinatra was born on 12 December 1915 and died on 15 May 1998. During his eighty-two years on this earth he structured a career that spanned six decades, became a cultural icon, movie star, business man and playboy, but above all he created a uniquely substantial body of recorded work, something like 18,000 recordings, many of which are lauded as performances of unparalleled textual and emotional depth. Impossible as it is for any single artist to embody all the popular music of the twentieth century, Sinatra came closest.

Big claims are made on his behalf: that he could raise pop artistry to a transcendent level; that his mastery of phrasing, rhythm, dynamics and, above all, interpretation, helped define how vocalists came to approach a song; that he changed not only how songs were performed but which songs were performed. He helped perfect the concept of the Great American Songbook, building up a repertoire of standards by the great American songwriters of the first half of the century and creating definitive versions of songs that came to be regarded as classics. He was by no means a modest man, yet he preferred a much simpler description of what he did. He was, he often insisted, a saloon singer.

According to Elwood P. Dowd, the hero of Mary Chase's play *Harvey* (perhaps better known through the film starring James Stewart), nobody ever brings anything small into a bar. Patrons tend to have large problems or big dreams, and over drinks in the wee hours they will share them with you. Sinatra shared some of those stories whenever he requested the audience 'assume the position of a bartender'. He called them 'saloon songs' or 'drunk songs', woeful tales of loss sung by a man who owned mansions with swimming pools and helipads, Learjets with piano bars.

They were heart-rending accounts of lonesomeness from an individual who was seldom alone and whose company could include some of the most glamorous and desirable men and women in the world. Yet he excelled at such songs and made the listener believe that he knew exactly how it felt to be one of the lost and the lonely.

'I've been around joints all my life. I've seen so many joints I should have been a chiropractor'; so said Frank's pal Joe E. Lewis, but it could easily have been Sinatra himself speaking. He knew the inside of a saloon from an early age. Sinatra, like many others, was of the opinion that Prohibition was the dumbest law in American history. He was adamant about this. 'I know what I'm talking about,' he would insist. 'I was there.'

The Volstead Act was introduced when Sinatra was just four years old and repealed when he was eighteen – formative years. Hoboken, his birthplace, had been one of the departure points for American troops heading into Europe during the First World War, and so drinking had been prohibited there even before Prohibition was extended nationwide. These restrictions had been routinely ignored, and when the Eighteenth Amendment became law in January 1920 the people of Hoboken largely chose to ignore this, too. Sinatra's father Marty, who had fought as a bantamweight in his youth, managed to get some muscle work with bootleggers, standing guard over some of the many trucks making booze runs. One night he returned home with his head bleeding, and his wife decided he needed another line of work. Dolly Sinatra organized the setting up of a saloon on the corner of 4th Street and Jefferson. It was called Marty O'Brien's.

Marty O'Brien was the name under which Sinatra senior had fought – Irish boxers being more popular than Italian fighters at the time – and, although it was nominally a restaurant, in reality it was a speakeasy. Nobody in their right mind, Sinatra himself pointed out, would go to a place called Marty O'Brien's to eat. It was young Frankie's first experience of a saloon and the first place he sang in public. There was a player-piano in the front room, and sometimes customers would hoist young Frankie on top of it to sing along with the music on the roll.

One day he was rewarded with a nickel, and he decided right then that singing was the racket for him.

Many years later he became known to friends as the Innkeeper, such was his hospitality; he was a constant plate-filler and glass-replenisher. He never tired of the ambience of a good joint. Touring with him late in his career Shirley MacLaine recalled that wherever they went after dinner would have to include a piano player and a bar – Sinatra's idea of home.

Rumours of gangster connections plagued Sinatra for much of his career. He had a standard response ready for journalists and Senate committees – he was an entertainer, he worked in certain types of establishments; some of these establishments might be owned and occasionally frequented by a certain class of businessman. 'I spent a lot of time working in saloons, and saloons', he pointed out, 'are not run by Christian Brothers. I didn't meet any Nobel Prize winners in saloons. But if Francis of Assisi had been a singer and working in saloons, he would've met the same guys.' These gentlemen ran good saloons, and when they paid you the cheques did not bounce. They might come backstage to thank you, you might swap hellos, you might even have a drink with them to be sociable, but that was it.

Up to a point this was true – gangsters ran a lot of speakeasies, and some of the money that came out of Prohibition went into nightclubs – but Sinatra had more than a nodding acquaintance with several mobbed-up types, some of whom he gladly called friends. He also had a regard for the likes of Lucky Luciano that was only just shy of hero worship. Prohibition not only helped the Mob forge alliances, establish power and generate huge amounts of capital; it was also regarded by many Americans as unjust, helping bootleggers achieve a sympathetic, almost romantic image, especially in places like New York's Little Italy. Many Italian immigrants, relative latecomers to America, saw themselves as a persecuted minority. They were often isolated and the victims of slurs and prejudices. The police were regarded with suspicion, and Sinatra himself developed a mistrust of cops after, he claimed, several incidences in adolescence of being stopped by beat officers who accused him of

Sinatra and Dean Martin share a joke with affiliate Rat Pack member 'Little Sister' Shirley MacLaine

having stolen the expensive clothes he was wearing – even then he was already a dandy, nicknamed 'Slacksey O'Brien' by contemporaries.

Gangsters, meanwhile, were local celebrities; they had new cars, flash clothes, beautiful companions. There were rumours that one of the chiefs of the New Jersey gangster confederacy, Waxy Gordon, drank regularly in Marty O'Brien's. Although Sinatra was adamant that he never saw him there, it was entirely possible. Dolly, the driving force in the Sinatra family, was in her element behind a bar. Garrulous, foul-mouthed and always busy, she had become a successful ward heeler for the local Democratic political boss. She spoke most of the Italian dialects in her neighbourhood, and everyone knew that if you were a poor immigrant who needed help with citizenship papers, employment, a welfare cheque or a food parcel she could arrange it. In return she would bully or cajole voters into returning favours during elections. Her political activities meant the saloon was unlikely ever to be closed, but many politicians had gangster connections, and even if she never came into direct contact with *the boys* through her political affiliations the illegal booze was supplied via the Mob.

Gangsters eventually began to replace cowboys on screen as Sinatra was growing up – Jimmy Cagney, Edward G. Robinson and George Raft. Raft became an early drinking buddy when Sinatra moved to Hollywood; they even swapped ties at Christmas. Years later, when Raft hit hard times, Sinatra issued him with a blank cheque (up to one million dollars) to help with unpaid taxes being sought by the Internal Revenue Service.

Raft had been taught his signature coin-flicking trick one night in the Brown Derby in Hollywood by a childhood friend from Hell's Kitchen. His friend was Benjamin 'Bugsy' Siegel, the man who went on to open up Las Vegas. Decades later, when Sinatra and other members of the Rat Pack played certain Vegas venues, it was sometimes at the behest of gangster owners. What were the Vegas rooms really? Just spiffed-up saloons.

Sinatra's innate clannishness was also partly a result of his upbringing, and in adulthood he was forever creating cohorts of trusted allies. He also dedicated himself to the avoidance of solitude – there were few things he loathed more than finding himself alone. Dolly's determination to better the family's social position meant she was perpetually busy. The Sinatras moved to nicer neighbourhoods, had a family Cadillac and were always relatively comfortable. Young Frank, however, was something of a latchkey kid. Between the ages of six and twelve he was usually looked after by his grandmother during the day. His mother was otherwise engaged, his father was notoriously taciturn, and, following his own difficult birth, he had no siblings to talk to or play with.

A single child was a rarity in Hoboken's Little Italy. As an adult he recalled how much he hated lying in the dark as a kid – 'a million things in your head and nobody to tell them to'. In later life he dreaded finding himself alone in the small hours because he believed that was when 'them devils come'. And so he ensured that there was always company, especially in the evenings. There was usually an eclectic mix behind the rope in the private room: film stars, fellow musicians, sportsmen and sports journalists, working girls, the occasional politician. There were also often several large men with colourful *noms de plume*. Some of the heavies with broken noses and pinkie rings could be deceptively intelligent, even witty; most were not. One or two might have been hired specifically by Sinatra to clear a path for him through the general public – comedian Don Rickles, a friend of Sinatra's, called them his 'tractors' – but there could also be fringe or even fully fledged hoodlums. One night in 1974, sitting in Jilly's, he looked up and observed, 'Jesus, there's about forty-three indictments right at the bar.' After the bars closed the party would move on to hotel rooms or houses, often his.

He hated sleeping before sun-up. His resilience was legendary, and he was inevitably the last man standing. Sometimes weary friends would organize rotas, taking turns to be the ones expected to stay the distance. Those who could not manage to keep up and who begged to be released were 'bums'.

America celebrated the occasion of Sinatra's eightieth birthday with a tribute concert held at the Shrine Auditorium in Los Angeles in November 1995. The great and the good of the entertainment industry gathered together to eulogize him and perform some of the songs he had made famous. Before he sang 'Angel Eyes', one of Sinatra's all-time favourite saloon songs, Bruce Springsteen told the audience, 'My first recollection of Frank's voice was coming out of a jukebox in a dark bar on a Sunday afternoon, when my mother and I went searching for my father.' His mother had stopped and told him, ' "Listen to that. That's Frank Sinatra. He's from New Jersey." ' Springsteen continued, 'It was the deep blueness of Frank's voice that affected me the most, and while his music became synonymous with black tie, good life, the best booze, women, sophistication, his blues voice was always the sound of hard luck and men late at night with the last ten dollars in their pockets trying to figure a way out.'

That so many people, mainly men, chose Sinatra to be some kind of patron saint of the lost, the last and the least was an achievement; something he could only manage because of the 'Fall'. Naturally before the Fall there was a spectacular, dizzying rise. Frank Sinatra began his career as a singer with the Harry James and Tommy Dorsey bands. He was popular, but nobody suspected that when he first set out on a solo career he would change the course of popular music.

Sinatra was booked as an 'Added Extra Attraction' for Benny Goodman, the 'King of Swing', for a four-week stint at the Paramount Theatre in New York, beginning on 30 December 1942. Sinatra's manager, George Evans, later admitted to having hired a dozen girls to swoon at Sinatra's performance, but hundreds more screamed louder. The audience response to the skinny, hollow-cheeked boy-singer was phenomenal, unprecedented – it marked the beginning of Sinatramania. He returned to the Paramount in October 1944. On Columbus Day, a school holiday, something like 30,000 youngsters queued to gain entrance to the theatre. Times Square was blocked. Over 200 policemen had to be redeployed from guard duty at the Columbus Day Parade to help control the crowds. In total 421 police reserves, twenty-six radio cars, two emergency trucks, four lieutenants, two inspectors, seventy patrolmen, fifty traffic cops, twelve mounted police, twenty policewomen and two hundred detectives were also required.

Sinatra had rapidly become Columbia Record's bestselling artist. He was a star of radio and had signed a movie deal with MGM, making his first film, *Higher and Higher*, in 1943. The press and most adults were flabbergasted at the hysteria he engendered. He was dubbed the 'Croon Prince of Swing', the 'Lean Lark' and the 'Sultan of Swoon'. Fan clubs sprang up nationwide – 2,000 of them – and 'bobbysoxers', as they had been christened by the press, lined up to see him clutching heart-shaped boxes of chocolates. They fought for the right to dig up his footprints in the snow and take them home to keep in the refrigerator; they hid in his dressing-room, hotel rooms, the trunk of his car; they screamed, fainted and wet their seats. America had seen nothing like it since Valentino, yet Sinatra was no Valentino. He was emaciated, vulnerable-seeming, with a shy, self-deprecating smile; he wore sweaters, bow ties and sports jackets. He was happily married, and the bobbysoxers loved Nancy, too. In terms of popular music he was the first teen idol and altered for ever the way audiences reacted to their heroes.

And then, the Fall.

It began with Ava. He was dancing with Lana Turner – one of his many extramarital indiscretions – in a nightclub in Palm Springs one night in 1947 when he was first properly introduced to Ava Gardner. They already knew of each other of course. Ava was only in her mid-twenties but had already been married and divorced twice – first to Mickey Rooney then to Artie Shaw. In many ways she was a female counterpart of Sinatra's. She loved sex and was promiscuous – her lovers in the late 1940s were said to have included the actors Robert Taylor, Howard Duff and Robert Mitchum, the singer Mel Tormé as well as Howard Hughes. She claimed never to have actually slept with Hughes, but he was obsessed with her, and she allowed him to court her. She was sexually adventurous, and on more than one occasion had demanded, and was granted, guided tours of upmarket brothels. She smoked heavily and blew smoke rings – an affection that annoyed Sinatra – could be crude, profane, even vulgar and had a reputation as a drinker. Mickey Rooney was able to confirm that she had a tremendous capacity for liquor. She was fond of champagne and drank it as though it were lemonade; she liked mixing beer and Scotch and loved trying cocktails, the more complex and potent the better.

In later life she recalled that many nights spent with Sinatra would begin with three large Martinis each, followed by wine at dinner and then drinking late into the night at clubs. She wondered how they had managed it. She was mercurial and prone to impulsive shifts of mood, including sudden explosive rages, even when stone-cold sober. Several ex-lovers and her former personal maid bore witness to the fact that alcohol often aggravated these inclinations; she once knocked Howard Hughes out with an ornamental vase.

In 1949 Sinatra and Gardner embarked on a turbulent affair. Friends warned him how dangerous it was; George Evans was frantic with worry, especially after the affair became an open secret, hinted at then exposed by the press. Sinatra was already, inevitably, losing his audience of bobbysoxers, and now they were smashing copies of 'Nancy (with the Laughing Face)' and sending the pieces in the post to gossip columnists. Those who knew him feared it wasn't just career suicide; it was an addictive, destructive passion capable of ruining many lives. There were insecurities and small and large infidelities on both sides: jealousies, recriminations, drink-fuelled rows and ardent reunions. Sinatra was sick with worry; he could only manage sleep with pills and booze.

It was torture for him to be apart from her but often intolerable when they were together. Ava swore she loved him, but she could be callous, cruel and indifferent towards him when she chose to be. 'It's killing me,' he told Hank Sanicola, his part-time manager, piano player and bodyguard. 'Little by little, man, I'm dying.' He was reduced to begging her, using emotional blackmail; there was at least one – apparently serious – suicide attempt.

His divorce from Nancy, which Ava had insisted upon, was finalized in November 1951, and a week later he and Ava were married. It did not save the relationship. Ava was a big star now, and Sinatra was on the slide. In the early 1950s he returned to the Paramount, but the crowds were considerably smaller. He played Chez Paree in Chicago, a

1,500-seater, and only 150 people came. His nightclub work dried up; venues became smaller and less salubrious; he was heckled by drunks. Even in Hoboken, where he played at a fire-fighters' fund-raiser, he was booed and had fruit thrown at him. He was dropped by Columbia, who claimed they couldn't give his records away. He lost his radio shows and his television programme, his films flopped, and he was released from contract. He had financial problems. He struggled to pay Nancy alimony and had to borrow money to pay outstanding taxes.

According to Ava, 'Nobody wanted to hang around him. He couldn't lift the bill, take people out, amuse them. There was nobody but me.'

He and Ava argued as they had done before the marriage, perhaps even more viciously. There were frequent separations and reunions. In early 1953 Ava flew to London from the set of *Mogambo* to have an abortion, her second in rapid succession. She told the press it was a miscarriage but years later admitted she had had a termination because at the time she hated Sinatra so much.

In October MGM announced that Gardner and Sinatra had 'exhausted every resource to reconcile their differences' and they were to separate. Ava had decided it was over. Three weeks later Frank slit his left wrist. He was discovered by Jimmy Van Heusen, who rushed him to hospital and told the press there had been an accident with a broken glass. Sinatra was desperate for reconciliation – he even used the same gossip columnists he usually despised to plead with her to return – but she was adamant. They did occasionally join together again briefly, but there would never be anything like a lasting reunion. She left him, and for a long time he hurt badly.

He lost virtually everything, but he fought his way back. He took on the role of Maggio in *From Here to Eternity* for a desultory fee and earned himself an Oscar in 1954. He signed with a new label, Capitol, on terms that reflected his low status – a one-year contract with no advance payment. He even had to pay his own studio costs – but went on to produce some of the best-regarded records in the history of popular music. After flying so high then plummeting so low he rebuilt himself and his career and took it to even greater heights.

His tribulations nearly destroyed him – especially his relationship with Ava, whom he always regarded as the love of his life – but they also gave him artistic capital and a new audience. Sinatra had been rejected for service during the war, classed 4F because of a punctured eardrum he acquired during his difficult birth. A lot of men, particularly serving men, had resented the fact that he not only sat out the conflict but spent the war years serenading America's young women. They were, however, willing to forgive Sinatra because he had been seen to suffer.

Ava had broken and walked all over his heart, and he had been stomped to death on film in *From Here to Eternity*, so when the former Sultan of Swoon sang 'Where Are You?' (his first stereo release) or lamented his fate 'In the Wee Small Hours of the Morning' they allowed that his melancholy might be authentic.

'It's always been just this little guy telling this story,' Ella Fitzgerald said of Sinatra's singing style, and with his classic Capitol albums of the 1950s he established the persona of the bruised romantic huddled on a barstool nursing a drink and smoking endless cigarettes. His voice now had a darker hue and timbre, a newfound maturity that allowed him to become a master of the drunken lament, the saloon ballad, the torch song. Nelson Riddle, probably his greatest collaborator, had a theory he often expounded. 'Ava did that to him,' Riddle maintained. 'It was Ava who taught him how to sing a torch song. She was the greatest love of his life, and he lost her.'

This new, grown-up Sinatra took time to develop, and as well as the sombre small-hours drinker he also eventually began displaying a cockiness that had been largely absent from his time as the boy-singer.

In 1954 it was the single 'Young at Heart', his first top-five single in eight years, that signalled the rejuvenation of his recording career, and it was followed by two ten-inch collections of upbeat standards – *Songs for Young Lovers* and *Swing Easy*. His first album proper for his new label, though, was *In the Wee Small Hours* a dark-toned collection of saloon songs that made clear his altered temperament. The boyishness had gone, something that was also evident in a change of visual image. There were no more bow ties and sweaters; now it was dark suits, snap-brimmed hats, raincoats. His album covers began to feature shadowy figures standing alone under a lamppost or at rest on a bar counter. People began to refer to his deliberately downbeat recordings as 'suicide songs', and Sinatra himself joked that the records came with a free gun – a water pistol filled with bourbon.

He would also soon show the world another persona, that of Pack Leader and Chairman of the Board. This was the Sinatra who refused the possibility of suffering and dangled the world on a string. 'Say, why don't we mix us up a little salad?' Dean Martin would suggest as he rolled the portable bar on stage in Vegas. It was known as the 'lunch cart' and was decorated with a sign that read: 'DON'T THINK – DRINK'. Although Dean played up his booze-hound reputation in public, in real life Sinatra always had the more ferocious appetites. Because he considered Dean to be his blood brother he – and only he – was allowed to duck out scandalously early in order to prepare for the following morning's golf. Everybody else would be required to carry on carousing until the Leader saw dawn rise, a signal to begin considering the possibility of sleep. Play-acting aside, Sinatra would boast about Dean, 'I spill more than he drinks.'

He was intemperate in all his passions and usually acted on them. Friends such as Shirley MacLaine talked diplomatically of his 'wide emotional landscape', but nobody seriously doubted that he was prone to the kind of emotional lurches and violent contradictions that were exacerbated by booze. A belligerent bartender might easily 'become punched' during an argument about the correct presentation of a Dry Martini; on the other hand, the time a busboy dropped a tray of glasses in his presence and was sacked on the spot Sinatra not only insisted that the man keep his job but paid for hundreds of dollars' worth of glasses for himself and the busboy to smash. His gratuities were legendary, but if he was presented with a sambuca with two or four coffee beans rather than the three required for luck the drink might easily end up on the wall.

There was a similar swaying of moods evidenced on his greatest recordings, which could veer from the cocky and exultant to the deeply melancholic and romantic. The set of albums he recorded for Capitol

'That's life!' Sinatra at the Royal
Albert Hall, London, 1989

in the 1950s – the cream of which are referred to by aficionados as 'the fabulous sixteen' – alternated between the playboy swagger of *Swing Easy!* or *Come Fly with Me* and the quiet desperation of *No One Cares* or *In the Wee Small Hours.*

When he was asked at a New York party in the mid-1970s what was his own favourite recording was, Sinatra immediately answered that it was *Only the Lonely*, and plenty of commentators would concur that it might well be his greatest moment. Arranger Nelson Riddle also nominated it as his own favourite vocal album – not least because he had a full week, much longer than usual, to work on his arrangements.

Originally conceived as a follow-up to 1956's *Where Are You?*, it was recorded in May and June of 1958. As with the best of his classic Capitol albums, it had a sustained theme, one of loss but also resignation and reflection. It also had a near-perfect selection of songs, beginning with the title track, by Sammy Cahn and Jimmy Van Heusen, especially commissioned by Sinatra for the album.

'You wanna call this "For Losers Only"?' Cahn was reputed to have joked after completing the song.

'Yeah,' Sinatra apparently replied. 'It's for all those losers who drink as hard as they feel.'

Frank Sinatra Sings for Only the Lonely, to give the album its full title, also contained two of the greatest ever saloon songs. 'Angel Eyes' had been written in 1953 by Matt Dennis for the film *Jennifer*. It had already been recorded by both Nat King Cole and Ella Fitzgerald, who once named it as her all-time favourite song, but quickly became associated with Sinatra. It was a drinking song with a chorus of 'Drink up all you people', and Sinatra adored the ending – ''Scuse me while I disappear' – so much so that for several years he would use the song to close his live concert appearances.

The other song was the one Sinatra described as the granddaddy of all saloon songs, 'One for My Baby (And One More for the Road)'. A saloon song in Sinatra's hands could become a Tin Pan Alley equivalent of the blues, an urban blues, late-night soliloquies told in a small dimly lit bar somewhere in the cold heart of a big city. Frank Sinatra Jr once called *Only the Lonely* the greatest blues album ever made, and 'One for My Baby' was its heart-rending climax.

Originally written by Harold Arlen and Johnny Mercer for Fred Astaire to perform in the 1943 film *The Sky's the Limit*, Ida Lupino reprised it in a 1948 film *Road House* around the same time Sinatra first recorded it himself in a sweetly balladic version arranged by Axel Stordahl. In 1955 Sinatra played opposite Doris Day in *Young at Heart* and sang a piano-and-vocal version of the song arranged and played by a young André Previn. But his definitive recording – *the* definitive version of the song – was made for *Only the Lonely* in 1958.

'One for My Baby' is, in Tin Pan Alley parlance, a 'tapeworm', the name given to any song exceeding the standard thirty-two-bar form. It is a difficult song, not just because of its length (forty-eight bars) but because of its key change. When he recorded it in 1947 Sinatra had sung it in B-flat ascending to D; in 1958 he raised it a whole tone, from C to E. Shifting the range actually heightened the fragility of his singing, which made dramatic rather than musical sense. It was a barstool lament told in the wee small hours, a hard-luck story poured out to a bartender where the singer lets us know that he has troubles but adheres to a code that means he can only tell so much.

The producer of the *Only the Lonely* sessions, Dave Cavanaugh, apparently decided to try to re-create an intimate nightclub atmosphere for the recording of 'One for My Baby' by switching off the studio lights, leaving just a single spot picking out Sinatra. Nelson Riddle's orchestration was fittingly minimal with muted strings providing a slow pulse, a backdrop against which Sinatra bunches together or draws out his phrasing, creating a slightly meandering, hesitant narrative. Most of the story is told with piano and voice. The pianist was Bill Miller, Sinatra's longest-serving and most *simpatico* piano player. Miller first played with Sinatra in the early 1950s after Jimmy Van Heusen heard him in the lounge of the Desert Inn and urged Frank to hire him. He accompanied Sinatra in his final year at Columbia and went on to play a crucial role in the classic recordings for Capitol and Reprise. He also appeared on stage with Frank all over the globe. Miller was perfect as the saloon-bar pianist, sounding as though he might be playing in a back room, perhaps even oblivious of Sinatra's presence. Riddle also added a broken alto-sax solo in the final chorus just as the voice is rising to a pained climax, quivering just shy of breaking before finally wandering off into the distance.

The finished version of piano and vocal was recorded in a single take. It might easily be Sinatra's finest ever performance, one that allowed him to use his skills as both singer and actor, bringing a compelling sincerity to the lyrics that perfectly conveyed a quiet desperation. It sounded like personal grief distilled into superb music.

His personal identification with this and other saloon songs was obvious. He knew about crushing defeat, heartfelt pain and loneliness. Even in the years when he was back on top, singing a lament about the loss of love, he could still feel the hurt and cry out the loneliness through the songs. He knew exactly what these songs were about. 'I've been there,' he would say; 'been there – and back.'

Sinatra also honed his performance of 'One for My Baby' to perfection in concert. He often began by explaining his role as the saloon singer and by introducing the story of a 'guy whose chick has split and left him in no mood to go out among us'. He would usually sing it just before the intermission, with the house lights lowered, sitting down or leaning against the piano with a glass and cigarette in his hand. Sometimes he would turn away from the microphone and walk away slowly during the final chorus, his last words barely audible as set off down the long, lonely road.

By the end of the 1950s he was resolutely back on top. In 1959 he heard that a friend, Skinny D'Amato, who had helped him out with gigs during the lean years, was having financial difficulties with his nightspot, the 500 Club in Atlantic City. Sinatra offered to play a stint there in the summer. His eight weeks at the 500 recalled some of the mayhem of the so-called 'Swoonatra' years. Police were required to try to control excited fans at both the club and his hotel. Reservations were sold on at 1,000-per-cent profit; one fan offered Sinatra fifty dollars for a cigarette butt he was about to discard; two hundred women were reported as needing hospital treatment as a result of the crushes.

There were, however, some crucial differences from the scenes years earlier. The first was that the female audience members were no longer bobbysoxers – the woman who hurled herself in front of Sinatra's limousine pleading, 'Run over me, Frankie! Run over me,' was in her forties. The second was that many in the audience were men. The teen idol who had been described by one New Jersey newspaper as the 'Fragile Finch' was now openly admired by other men. He had paid his dues, and his response to his troubles had been to fight back. He was allowed to express his regrets, and a generation (and more) of males allowed that he had done it gracefully and in a manly fashion.

When Frank Sinatra passed away in 1998 it was inevitable that one particular song would be singled out for use in discussion of his art and life. That song was 'My Way' – and it was the wrong song. Written by Gillis Thibault, Jacques Revaux and Claude François, its original French title had been 'Comme d'habitude' ('As Usual'), and it had been a European hit for François. It was Paul Anka, himself a former teen idol, who conceived an English lyric with Sinatra specifically in mind and passed it on through Don Costa, a producer who had worked with both men. It was musically uninspiring, rhythmically dull and plodding with very little in the way of melodic content, and the lyric lacked any real subtlety or wit. Sinatra had to be talked into recording it and devoted no more than half an hour to it during a studio session in December 1968.

Released as a single, it only just scraped into the Billboard charts, peaking at number 27, but reached number 4 in the UK and remained in the British charts for 122 weeks. When it was first included in live performances it received only polite applause, but gradually the song seeped into public consciousness, and sheet-music sales eventually reached one million. It became a key part of Sinatra's mythology – a song that was a metaphor for his own life, lived without apology, a defiant autobiography. Sinatra himself remained, at least for a time, ambivalent about the song. He was barely in his mid-fifties when he recorded it and hated the idea that any sort of end was near. He once said that every time he got up to sing 'My Way' he gritted his teeth because no matter what his image was he hated boastfulness. He understood it was a hymn to boastfulness, self-aggrandizement and surly arrogance. Yet the public grew to expect it, and it became a major part of his performances in the last two decades of his career, with Sinatra himself eventually declaring it his own personal anthem and bellowing it out in rock stadiums and amphitheatres, venues not really suited for saloon songs. He must have at times regretted such a close association with a song that could have been one that Hitler might have sung as he marched into Paris, and the self-mythologizing came back to haunt him when Kitty Kelley called her critical biography *His Way*.

Better and kinder to remember a different Sinatra. He first announced his retirement in 1971, and what was supposedly meant to be his final public appearance was a benefit concert in June at the Los Angeles Music Center. At the close of the show he told the audience that he had built his career on saloon songs and that he wanted to end quietly on such a song. He ordered the lights lowered, a single pin spot picked him out in silhouette, and he began singing 'Angel Eyes'. Towards the end he lit a cigarette and let the smoke wreathe around him, and after uttering the final line – ''Scuse me while I disappear' – he was gone. By many accounts it was a stunning moment to witness on stage.

He returned, of course, but even the most ardent fan would concede that his work from then on was flawed, often ill-conceived, sometimes embarrassingly awful, with fewer and fewer of the touches of genius so apparent in the 1950s and 1960s. The Sinatra who should count was the one who called himself 'the Last Saloon Singer', the one who settled himself on a barstool and told the crowd, 'This is the part of the programme where we sing a drunk song. Drunk songs are usually done in small bars in the wee hours of the morning, usually talked or sung by a fellah who's got problems like his broad flew the coop. With another guy and all the bread.

'So, if you will assume the position of a bartender . . .'

EXIT

The Last Saloon Singer – Sinatra performs
under a spotlight, 1970. 'If you will
assume the position of a bartender . . .'

Sinatra and Dean Martin mix drinks on stage at the Sands

Some Notes on the Particulars

MEASURE FOR MEASURE

Ah, the particulars. They're complicated – or can be. Researching these recipes (it's thirsty work, but . . .) it became obvious how many subtle, and often not so shaded, differences there are in the instructions for preparing cocktails. Some recipes direct you to use jiggers, ponies, shots, dashes and splashes; others lists ingredients as parts or measures; the most precise read like mathematical formulas listing quantities in fluid ounces or millilitres.

Cocktail-making is not, however, a branch of science, rocket or otherwise – or it shouldn't be. The cocktail is by definition a mixed drink, and the essence of the cocktail is the ratio of ingredients (four parts gin to one part vermouth), whatever the individual measurable quantities. I took the decision here to make these recipes as simple as possible to comprehend and reproduce. For this reason, rather than specify precise US, imperial or metric quantities, I have described the recipes in *measures*.

A measure is based on the large cup of a standard American double jigger. The jigger is simple, elegant, functional and an absolutely essential part of any home cocktail kit, a durable, metal (usually stainless steel), double-ended measuring cup that rests snugly between the fingers and allows the user to pour out standard measures. The two conical cups are linked at their bases – one up, one down – one cup being half the volume of the other. They are available in various sizes, usually starting with 1 US fluid oz. and ½ US fluid oz. cups. (British jiggers use metric measurements and begin at 25 ml and 50 ml). The larger cup should be considered a *single measure*; turn it over, and the smaller cup is a *half measure*. For recipes that use ¾ measures use the larger cup and judge by eye. Using this system means that you can achieve precision and consistency without having to resort to complicated equations and conversions.

Cocktails are also a matter of personal taste. If you decide you would like stronger or weaker versions then jiggers come in graduated sizes, adjust the drinks as you see fit – just be sure to maintain the all-important ratios.

Talking of personal taste, there is only the most general agreement on many cocktail recipes. For the recipes I collected and collated here I used two basic principles for inclusion:

(1) that they should be drinks that Sinatra (and/or associates) were known to have enjoyed;
(2) that they should be historically authentic.

I tried to collect as many of the recipes as I could from vintage books, articles and menu cards. For me (and for many other fans and commentators) the classic Sinatra era was from the early/mid-1950s into the early 1960s. For this reason I have focused on versions of drinks as they were served during those times. Of course, the true classics are timeless and most were formulated much earlier, but cocktails evolve and mutate, for better or worse – these days usually for the worse. Even the most established classics – perhaps especially the classic cocktails – have different schools of thought concerning their proper construction, but I chose to err on the side of simplicity and popularly accepted standards, as prescribed by respected experts in the field of mixology. In the end it's a personal judgement, but I regard the versions of drinks in this book to be if not definitive then as close to trustworthy as it was in my power to make them.

BAR EXAM

Movers and Shakers

Aside from a jigger measure, the other absolutely essential component of any home mixologist's kit is the cocktail shaker. Available in a variety of shapes, sizes and materials (from plastic to cut-glass crystal and silver), a shaker must have a large opening for ice and a small one for pouring. Decent basic shakers are widely available from most large retailers and are usually reasonably priced. Secondhand or vintage shakers are probably the more expensive option, but there is no shortage of originals for sale online, and searching charity or antique shops can occasionally pay dividends.

In March 2014 Al Capone's cocktail shaker was put up for auction at Sotheby's. Listed as a 'communion flagon in silver plate with detachable cover', the provenance was described as 'By repute given to Mr Alphonse Capone by some of his associates as a Christmas gift'. It was inscribed 'To a Regular Guy from the Boys. 1932'. The estimate was between £1,000 and £1,500. It eventually sold for £50,000.

If your budget cannot stretch that far, the most common, popular and perfectly serviceable cocktail shakers are the Manhattan, the French and the Boston.

Most people will be familiar with the classic polished-steel shaker usually known as the Manhattan, or sometimes the cobbler shaker, a three-piece shaker consisting of lid/cap (which sometimes doubles up as a measure), built-in strainer and main body.

The French shaker is a more basic two-piece, consisting of a metal bottom and cap. It often requires the use of a clip-on strainer when dealing with cubed or crushed ice.

The Boston shaker is a two-piece consisting of an outer steel 'tin' and a slightly smaller inner mixing glass made of hardened glass. When the glass is inserted inside the tin a seal is created, allowing the ingredients to be shaken. As with the French shaker, the Boston often requires the use of a separate strainer.

Once you have your double-ended measuring cup, your shaker, your bottles and plenty of ice on hand you can begin mixing some basic recipes. There are still, however, some other items of bar equipment that may be required on a regular basis. These include:

A strainer – a metallic-mesh strainer that clips on to shakers or mixing glasses/pitchers to prevent ice entering the finished drink; commonly known as a Hawthorne Strainer.

A mixing glass/pitcher – Manhattans and traditional Martinis are stirred not shaken and best prepared in a large mixing glass. The vessel should have a moulded lip for ease of pouring, and you should ensure in advance that your strainer fits snugly.

A long-handled bar spoon – this can have more than one function: as well as being used to stir drinks it can be used to measure out teaspoons of sugar, for example.

A glass or plastic stirring rod – not simply for those purists who fear that a bar spoon might impart a metallic taste to a drink; metal also has a tendency to collapse bubbles, and so a glass rod should be used for drinks requiring a fizz.

A muddler – a heavy, round-based wooden stick for mashing sugar and bitters in drinks such as the Old Fashioned; muddling releases oils and flavourings.

An ice bucket – not strictly necessary, but a vintage ice bucket can alleviate the need for constant trips to the freezer drawer and be aesthetically pleasing.

Glassware

Modern glasses tend to be significantly bigger than mid-twentieth-century glassware, especially the Martini glass. An Old Fashioned glass from the 1950s or 1960s would have a typical volume of 4–6 fluid oz.; the contemporary glass is more likely to be 6–8, sometimes even 12–13 fluid oz. A Highball glass of the time would hold between 8–10 fluid oz., but now it would be 12–14 fluid oz. The typical Cocktail glass of the mid-part of the last century would hold between 2–3½ fluid oz., but today the capacity is more typically 8–9 fluid oz.

As with cocktail shakers, original glassware, if your finances will allow it, can be found in junk and antique shops or on the internet (treasures such as original sets of Toot Shor's bar glasses are occasionally available online). Modern glassware is affordable, easily available and perfectly acceptable, even if much of it lacks the aesthetic beauty of older glasses. In strictly practical terms most cocktails can be served in any available, clean, unbroken vessel. If, however, the look is important and correct and proper presentation considered crucial to enjoyment (the type of high standards Sinatra usually demanded) then it only requires a little effort to ensure that your cocktail is accommodated in an appropriate glass.

The classic categories include:

Old fashioned – the squat, heavy-bottomed tumbler built to withstand the onslaught of muddling required for an Old Fashioned or a Caipirinha; it also the vessel of choice for serving a Whiskey Sour. It is also sometimes known as a Lowball or Rocks glass; it has a generous capacity for ice cubes.

Highball – the chimney-style glass used for taller drinks; also sometimes referred to as the Delmonico (shorter) or Collins (tallest). It is for use with drinks that are topped up with sodas or juices, such as the Cuba Libre, Bossa Nova or Ramos Gin Fizz.

Cocktail glass – a general nomenclature for a stemmed glass used to serve a mixed drink. Shape and size can vary enormously, but the main defining feature is the stem. Since the majority of cocktails should be served chilled, an elongated stem keeps the bowl clear of the heat of the hand. Both the Martini glass and the Margarita glass could be classed as cocktail glasses, although both have distinctive features of their own. The Martini glass is instantly recognizable because of its V-shaped bowl, while the Margarita is a larger variant of the champagne saucer and sometimes described as looking like an inverted sombrero.

Champagne flute – a slim, elegant container, perfect for a Bellini or Black Velvet. Champagne cocktails can also be served in the champagne saucer, also called a coupe, which, despite an enduring urban myth, was not modelled on one of Marie Antoinette's breasts.

Hurricane glass – a large, lamp-shaped glass, or goblet, which can be used for more exotic cocktails, such as the Blue Hawaii, because of its capacity to accommodate straws, fruit and other embellishments.

With time, patience, practice and experimentation you should eventually acquire the mixing, stock-keeping and acquisition skills required to service your own perfect home bar.

SOME TOASTS: TRADITIONAL SINATRA SALUTES

It's post time, ladies and gentlemen.
Here's to the confusion of our enemies.
Absent friends – fuck 'em.
Drink up and be somebody.
May you live to be a hundred, and may the last voice you hear be mine.

'Somebody up there likes me.'
Pointing to the heavens, 1970

Sammy Davis Jr, Dean Martin and Sinatra at the Cocoanut Grove, Los Angeles, for Eddie Fisher's opening night in 1961. The trio eventually took to the stage for a mini-Summit, amusing themselves but annoying some members of Fisher's audience and, for the first time, receiving unfavourable comments in the press. Note the Jack Daniel's bottle on the table.

Jack Daniel's Original Test Pilot

The entertainer Jackie Gleason was a large man who contained multitudes. In the USA, his homeland, he was known simply as the 'Great One', king of the small screen and star of *The Honeymooners* and *The Jackie Gleason Show*.

He made forays on to the big screen and was Oscar-nominated for the role of Minnesota Fats in *The Hustler*. He also played the comic sheriff Buford T. Justice in the *Smokey and the Bandit* films. He was a dedicated drinker – 'A man must always defend his wife, his family and his Martini' – and philanderer, wrote a ballet, designed clothes, jewellery and children's games. He was an early ufologist with a library of books on the subject and a home in the Catskills designed to look like a downed flying saucer.

He was also an unlikely musical star, and throughout the 1950s he oversaw the release of eighteen albums, most of which were bestsellers. Although he had no formal musical training he conducted his own hand-picked orchestras (eschewing technical terms such as pizzicato in favour of descriptions such as 'the sound of pissing off a high bridge into a teacup') and often composed (one-fingeredly on the piano) his own songs, including his theme tune, 'Melancholy Serenade'. Although largely forgotten now, his *Jackie Gleason Presents* series represented an early form of concept album, although the volume entitled *Music to Change Her Mind* could sum up the main concept: most of these records were marketed as aural seduction aids. 'The only thing better than one of my songs', he regularly boasted, 'is one of my songs with a glass of

Scotch.' *Lover's Portfolio* – described in the liner notes as 'music for listenin', sippin', dancin' and lovin'' – even came with a bartender's recipe manual. The first of the albums, *Music for Lovers Only*, was released in 1953 and reached number 1 in the charts and remained in top spot for seventeen weeks, keeping the likes of Sinatra, Doris Day, Perry Como, Nat King Cole, Frankie Laine, Kay Starr and Eddie Fisher at bay. The strangest record in the series was undoubtedly *Lonesome Echo*, which was a collaboration with Salvador Dalí.

Whatever Jackie Gleason's achievements as an innovator in mood music were, however, they were dwarfed by the contribution he made in facilitating one of the most significant partnerships in twentieth-century popular music: he introduced a young Frank Sinatra to Jack Daniel's. Before that night in a bar off Broadway in the early 1940s Sinatra had, like many callow youths, toyed with the occasional malt whisky in an attempt to appear sophisticated. This had not suited him, but as soon as he tasted Jack he was smitten.

It was the beginning of a life-long love affair, and Jack Daniel's inspired a devotion that most of the women in his life would have envied. Sometime in the 1960s Sinatra, it seems, suffered for a while with some kind of erectile dysfunction. Consulting a doctor he was told that his drinking could well be a contributing factor. Sinatra apparently told the doctor, 'If I gotta choose between getting loaded and getting my bird up, fuck it, I'm getting loaded.' The music came first, always, but drink appeared to be a close second, and Jack Daniel's was his constant companion. He took pains to ensure that a bottle would always be close at hand, his home bar was always stocked plentifully, bottles were required backstage at every performance, and he even kept ten cases on standby in the holds of his private jets, mindful of the fact that certain places he visited might not be as civilized as his home country.

The love affair was no secret – legends, stories and anecdotes abounded. He was known to friends as 'Jack Daniel's Original Test Pilot', and the *Washington Post* christened him the 'Bourbon Baritone'. He had a blazer with the Jack Daniel's crest on the breast pocket and a flag with the JD insignia. (Quincy Jones recalled being highly amused to see the flag featuring the famous bottle fluttering outside the compound on his first visit to Sinatra's Twin Palms mansion.) He was even named by the distillery as one of the Tennessee Squires, an elite group of aficionados – that also included Paul Newman, Elizabeth Taylor and J. Edgar Hoover – who were all granted their own plot of land on the original distillery site. The others received a square foot, but Sinatra was given a full acre. By the end of his life he owned millions in real estate, but that single plot of land was his proudest possession.

Sinatra himself liked to tell the story of his first visit to another doctor. The doctor quizzed him about his alcohol intake. He answered immediately, unblinking, 'I have thirty-six drinks a day.' The doctor asked him to be serious. Frank explained, seriously, that he drank a bottle of Jack Daniel's a day and figured he got about thirty-six shots to a bottle. The pinch-mouthed doctor wanted to know how he felt in the mornings. 'I don't know,' he replied. 'I'm never up in the morning, and I'm not sure you're the doctor for me.'

A photograph that amused him greatly was one mocked up by his friend, the Hollywood photographer Phil Stern. It featured a loose-limbed Sinatra floating in a jar on a shelf at Harvard Medical School. The label on the jar read:

SPECIMEN: F. Sinatra
SOLUTION: J. Daniel's

As soon as he saw it he phoned Stern and ordered a dozen copies.

There are many anecdotes and references to Jack Daniel's place in Sinatra's life. When Dean Martin sang a specially reworked version of 'You're the Tops' at one of Frank's birthday celebrations the lyrics included the lines:

He's the boy
Who wrote all the manuals.
On the joys
Of consuming Daniel's.

While filming *Meet Danny Wilson* in 1951 he had frequent forthright differences of opinion with co-star Shelley Winters. One day's shooting ended early after Winters punched Sinatra and stormed off set. When the cameras began rolling again the following day Sinatra was supposed to finish a scene with the line, 'I'll have a cup of coffee and leave you two lovebirds alone.' He chose to amend his dialogue and announced instead, 'I'll have a cup of Jack Daniel's, or I'm going to pull that blonde broad's hair out by its black roots.' Shooting was delayed again.

A Hawaiian club owner remembered him coming into his premises with a party of eight. He ordered a bottle of Jack Daniel's but then quickly called the waiter back and changed his order to one bottle each for everyone in the party. All eight bottles were finished before he left.

David Niven, in his autobiography *The Moon's a Balloon*, described a Fourth of July aboard Humphrey Bogart's yacht that culminated with Sinatra, accompanied by Jimmy Van Heusen, serenading guests until sunrise. On top of the piano was a bottle of Jack Daniel's which Frank gradually emptied.

Lena Samuels, a Vegas showgirl who was one of Sinatra's myriad conquests, said that when they kissed he tasted of Camel cigarettes, Jack Daniel's and mouthwash (he was known to be fastidious in his personal hygiene).

George Jacobs, who was employed as his personal valet for years, recalled in his memoir *Mr S.* how in the mid-1950s, just as his great comeback was beginning and during one of the very few quiet periods of social activity, Sinatra would require him to sit up late into the night playing cards. Sinatra would talk for hours on end about his career plans while working his way through a bottle of Jack.

Jacobs also described an incident in the early 1960s when Sinatra was planning to use the writer Albert Maltz to script a film based on William Bradford Huie's book about the only US military execution for desertion since the American Civil War, *The Execution of Private Slovik*. It was a potentially controversial project, and Maltz – one of the original Hollywood Ten blacklisted in the McCarthy witch-hunts – was a controversial choice, but Sinatra wanted to direct and had Oscar hopes.

He took out advertisements in the trade papers defending his right to make his own movies and employ whom he liked, but after a phone call from Joseph Kennedy berating him for stirring up 'commie Jew shit' that might damage his son's presidential campaign by association Frank unhappily abandoned the project. He was so frustrated at having to do so that, according to Jacobs, he went on a three-day Jack Daniel's binge and totally destroyed his office.

It is no surprise that his favourite drink was also name-checked in one of his most famous remarks, that he was for anything that helped a person through the night, whether it be prayer, tranquillizers or a bottle of Jack Daniel's. It has been suggested that the remark, which featured in a 1963 *Playboy* interview, was actually the work of Mike Shore, an executive at Sinatra's record company Reprise, but, wherever it originated, it was a true expression of a Sinatra credo.

Shortly after his death many fans made a pilgrimage to the site at 415 Monroe Street where the house he was born in had once stood. The sidewalk around the commemorative plaque was littered with offerings – loaves of Italian bread and bottles of Jack Daniel's. His daughter Nancy also ensured that there was a bottle of what he often described as 'a gentleman's drink' placed in the pocket of his funeral suit.

HOW SINATRA TOOK HIS

In an Old-Fashioned glass with a splash of branch water ('I'm thirsty, not dirty,' he once chided an overenthusiastic bartender), with just one or two rocks of ice – 'I'm drinking not skating.'

Sinatra backstage at the Sands in 1965 partaking of the liquid he often referred to as 'gasoline' while waiting to go on with the Count Basie Orchestra

CLASSIC BOURBON COCKTAILS

MANHATTAN

2 measures of rye, bourbon or Tennessee whiskey
½ measure of sweet (red) vermouth
2–3 dashes of Angostura bitters
1 maraschino cherry

Pour the liquid ingredients into a mixing glass filled with ice. Stir well and then strain into a chilled Cocktail glass. Garnish with the cherry.

For many years this classic cocktail – sometimes called the 'King of Cocktails' – was popularly supposed to have originated at the Manhattan Club in New York some time in the 1870s and was thought to have first been drunk at a party hosted by Winston Churchill's mother Jenny. The Churchill connection now seems unlikely, and a version of the drink was most probably served in the 1860s in at least one Broadway bar. The maraschino cherry appeared after 1900. Common variations include the Dry Manhattan, which uses dry as opposed to sweet vermouth and is served with a twist of citrus zest, and the Perfect Manhattan, a mixture of equal measures of dry and sweet vermouth garnished with a lemon twist. The Dry was a drink much favoured by almost all of the Vegas Rat Packers.

There is a story about Sinatra and this particular cocktail that is especially illustrative of his general temperament. In 1948 RKO wanted Sinatra to attend a première in San Francisco of his film *The Miracle of the Bells*. Aware that the film had already been savaged by several critics and was generally considered something of a flop, Sinatra was reluctant. When the studio pressed him he exacted revenge by arriving with a small entourage and set about systematically abusing RKO's charge account. He took a party of twenty-two people to four nightclubs and then returned to his hotel suite to party until 7 a.m.; he gifted cashmere sweaters, silk ties and handmade shirts to his entourage, and he hired a piano to be delivered to his room at 4 a.m., all of it paid for by RKO. It was evidence of his petulance and a lifelong hatred of being told what to do. The first thing he had done after checking himself into the largest suite in the Fairmont Hotel was to phone room service and place an order for eighty-eight Manhattans. When the carts full of cocktails began to arrive, he told the waiters, 'Just put them over there in the corner.' At the end of his stay the carts were removed, and not one drink had been sipped.

OLD FASHIONED

3 measures of rye, bourbon or Tennessee whiskey 1 sugar cube 2 dashes of Angostura bitters 2 orange slices 1 maraschino cherry	*Place the sugar cube at the bottom of an Old Fashioned glass, saturate with bitters, add one orange slice and muddle. Add ice cubes to the glass and pour the whiskey over. Stir well with a bar spoon and garnish with the second orange slice and cherry, secured to the orange slice with a toothpick.*

The Old Fashioned glass, named after the drink, is a squat tumbler with a capacity of around 8–12 fluid oz. Also referred to as a Lowball or Rocks glass, it was Sinatra's drinking vessel of choice.

Another classic bourbon cocktail, the Old Fashioned was served originally at the Pendennis Club, Louisville, Kentucky, around 1880 and may well have been the first drink to be commonly referred to as a 'cocktail'. It was Colonel James E. Pepper, a Pendennis Club member and bourbon distiller, who introduced it to the wider world via New York's Waldorf-Astoria bar. It was nominated by David A. Embury as one of the Six Basic Drinks in his 1948 book *The Fine Art of Mixing Drinks*.

The practice of adding sugar and fruit to alcoholic drinks, thereby creating a cocktail, is thought to have become commonplace during Prohibition and was usually done to try to mask the taste of dubious base spirits. Several pre-Prohibition recipes for Old Fashioneds did, however, include sugar, oranges or orange bitters and lemon peel – the cherry is a more recent addition. Modern Old Fashioneds are usually topped off with

soda water, a practice that is frowned upon by some traditionalists, although
even the earliest recipes allowed that water – usually plain branch water –
could be used to fully dissolve the sugar before adding the whiskey, since
undissolved sugar at the bottom of the glass can mar a drinker's final sip.

WHISKEY SOUR

3 measures of rye,
bourbon or Tennessee
whiskey
2 measures of fresh
lemon juice
1 measure of gomme
syrup
1 orange wheel
1 maraschino cherry
1 dash of egg white
(optional)

*Pour the whiskey, lemon juice and gomme
syrup into a cocktail shaker and stir to
dissolve. Add ice and shake well. Strain into
an Old Fashioned glass filled with ice cubes;
garnish with orange wheel and cherry. If
the egg white is to be included it should be
mixed with the other liquid ingredients in
the shaker.*

Like many legendary cocktails, the Whiskey Sour boasts a colourful
back story that may or may not be historically accurate. An Englishman
named Elliot Stubb in 1872, it is said, devised the Sour in a bar in Iquique,
then in Peru and now in Chile. Stubb had been a steward aboard a sailing
ship named *Sunshine* but had disembarked there in order to pursue his
dream of opening his own bar. Intent on creating a new speciality of the
house he experimented with a variety of ingredients before hitting on an
aperitif that made use of bourbon whiskey and the juice of the *limón de
Pica*, a small local lime grown in profusion at a nearby oasis. This new
'Sour', as he christened his invention, soon became popular in many of
the bars and social clubs around the port, and variations on it spread
throughout the world.

Sours, however – a base spirit mixed with citrus fruit and a sweetener
– were among the earliest-recorded cocktails, and Jerry Thomas – a star
mixologist regarded as the father of American cocktail culture – had already
included six basic sour recipes in his seminal tome *The Bar-Tender's Guide*

(How to Mix Drinks), which was first published in 1862, ten years before Stubb jumped ship.

Both the Old Fashioned and the Manhattan owe something to the sour tradition, and other cocktails with different base spirits and sweeteners, such as the Daiquiri (rum and lime juice) or the Cosmopolitan (vodka, cranberry and lime), are based on the same principle and so might also be considered part of the same family.

WARD 8

1 measure of rye, bourbon or Tennessee whiskey ½ measure of fresh lemon juice ½ measure of orange juice 1 measure of grenadine 1 maraschino cherry	*Pour all liquid ingredients into a cocktail shaker filled with ice. Shake vigorously and strain into a chilled Cocktail glass. Garnish with the cherry.*

In 1934 the Ward 8 was voted one of the ten best cocktails of the year by *Esquire Magazine*. Tradition has it that this cocktail originated in Boston in 1898 to celebrate the election of a local Democratic politician. That the politician in question was considered a dubious character might be inferred from the fact that he arranged his celebration party the night before the vote took place. A rival story claims the drink was invented in New York under similar circumstances, the area in question being well known for political corruption. Both tales would probably have appealed to Sinatra's mother Dolly, a well-known political fixer and ward heeler for the mainly Irish local Democratic party.

The Ward 8 is another direct descendant of the Whiskey Sour and is sometimes named as the traditional drink of the Scots Guards regiment of the British Army.

ALGONQUIN COCKTAIL

1½ measures of rye, bourbon or Tennessee whiskey

¾ measure of dry (white) vermouth

¾ measure of pineapple juice

Fill a cocktail shaker with ice, add all ingredients and shake vigorously for several minutes. Strain into a chilled Cocktail glass.

The Algonquin Hotel at 59 West 44th Street, Manhattan, opened in 1902 and eventually gained a reputation for hosting literary and theatrical notables. The most famous group of wits to meet there regularly became known as the 'Algonquin Round Table', although they also dubbed themselves the 'Vicious Circle'. Among the writers and critics who convened for lunch most days between 1919 and 1923 were George S. Kauffman, Alexander Woollcott, Dorothy Parker and Robert Benchley.

Much of the relentless trading of *bon mots* and trenchant, pithy comment (which helped fuel much poetry, column inches and theatrical dialogue) was drink-related. Dorothy Parker's contributions included 'OK, just one, seeing as we're up', and 'One more drink, and I'll be under the host', while Robert Benchley is fondly remembered for the immortal 'I must get out of these wet clothes and into a Dry Martini.'

WHISKEY SOUR IN THE ROUGH

1 measure of bourbon

2 quarters of fresh orange

2 quarters of fresh lemon

1 spoonful of sugar

Muddle the sugar, orange and lemon in a large Old Fashioned glass. Shake the bourbon briskly with cracked ice, strain into the glass and serve.

This was a cocktail available at the Flamingo Hotel and Casino, a venue that was a key part of Bugsy Siegel's grand dream for transforming Las Vegas into a gambling resort. When it opened, in December 1946, the 105-room luxury hotel, with its baroque interior and tuxedo-clad waiting staff, was the first of its kind on the Las Vegas Strip. Siegel named it in honour of his girlfriend, Virginia Hill, whose long and slender legs had earned her the pet name 'Flamingo'.

Siegel had predicted great things when persuading his fellow mobsters to invest in the hotel, and he was eventually proved right, yet on its grand opening – which drew stars such as Clark Gable, George Raft, Lana Turner, Judy Garland and Jimmy Durante – it was thought to be a folly; even worse, a flop. Siegel paid dearly for the hotel's failure to generate income rapidly enough to satisfy its investors (he was also suspected of skimming significant amounts from the $6 million construction costs) and was assassinated by the boys.

Gangster affiliations are a thing of the past, and the Flamingo, now owned by Caesars Entertainment, proved to be one of the great survivors of the original Vegas scene. These days the star attractions are more family-orientated, with residencies from the likes of Donny and Marie Osmond.

Scenes for Elvis's *Viva Las Vegas* were filmed in the hotel, and it was used in both the original *Oceans 11* and the remake.

BOB HOPE'S RYE LEMONADE

1 measure of rye whiskey
Fresh lemonade

Prepare an Old Fashioned glass by rubbing the rim with a lemon, sprinkling sugar over it and then placing in a refrigerator to chill for at least half an hour. Add rye, freshly made lemonade and ice to taste.

It was inevitable that Sinatra and Hope should be in each other's orbits, not least because of their mutual friend Bing. They shared the bill on several United Service Organizations tours and took turns guesting on their respective radio shows. They also appeared on one another's television shows. In fact, Sinatra's first television appearance was on a 1950 Bob Hope special, *The Star-Spangled Review*. Sinatra performed only one song, 'Come Rain or Come Shine', but also took part in sketches. He donned comedy ears and a pipe to play Bing in a parody of one of the

Crosby–Hope *Road to . . .* movies. Twelve years later he and Dean made a brief cameo appearance in the final *Road* film, *Road to Hong Kong.* Sinatra always remained grateful to Hope for allowing him the chance to appear in front of the nation at a time when nobody wanted to give him work.

The recipe, such as it is, was Hope's contribution to an *Esquire Drink Book.*

BENNY GOODMAN'S ADMIRAL COCKTAIL

1 measure of bourbon 2 measures of dry vermouth Juice of half a lemon	*Mix all liquid ingredients in a shaker filled with ice. Pour into an Old Fashioned glass and garnish with a single lemon twist.*

When Sinatra appeared with Benny Goodman, the King of Swing, at New York's Paramount Theatre at the end of December 1942 the hysterical reaction from his fans signalled a change in the course of popular music.

Sinatra was billed simply as an 'Extra Added Attraction', and Goodman was barely aware of him, despite his time with Tommy Dorsey. He introduced the young singer with a laconic 'And now, Frank Sinatra.' He had his back to the audience as Sinatra strode on stage, and the bobbysoxers erupted into a deafening roar. He turned around, looked at the crowd and asked, astonished, 'What the hell is that?'

What Goodman did not realize at the time was that that morning marked the beginning of the end of the Swing Era, the demise of the big bands and the rise of the singer.

Sinatra later remarked that he had learned an important lesson from Goodman about never taking his talent for granted. Goodman was a huge star, but the young Sinatra noticed that whenever he saw Goodman backstage he always seemed to be practising with his clarinet. If he wasn't blowing the thing he was engrossed in fingering it. When Sinatra asked him why he replied, 'Because if I'm not great, I'm good.'

'That stuck in my head,' said Sinatra.

TOOTS SHOR'S

His town. His Saloon.

Toots Shor's, the place 'where all the good guys went'

That was the legend attached to Bernard 'Toots' Shor, whose restaurant and lounge at 51 West 51st Street in Manhattan was a much-celebrated and highly renowned watering hole in the 1940s and 1950s. It was nominally a restaurant, but the food was never much more than standard sports-bar fare (shrimp cocktail, steak and baked potato). The true attractions were an oversized circular bar, Toots himself and a star clientele. It conspicuously lacked the elegance and refinement supposedly embodied in the Stork Club, El Morocco or the 21 Club but had equal kudos as one of the places to be seen in. It was a bar with the ambience of a men's club, the air thick with cigar smoke and casual profanities. 'Broads' were tolerated but wives usually frowned upon. It was the haunt of sports stars, actors, newspapermen, politicians and musicians from the jazz clubs of the nearby West 50s. Regulars included baseball giants Mickey Mantle and Joe DiMaggio along with Judy Garland, Ernest Hemingway, the well-known trial attorney Edward Bennett Williams and future Chief Justice Earl Warren.

Being famous, however, was no guarantee of special service. Both Charlie Chaplin and Louis B. Mayer complained at having to wait in line for tables but were given short shrift by Toots. One of the apparent attractions for celebrities was Shor's reputation for directing the needle at the great and the good. His quips, put-downs and jibes were legendary, and to be personally insulted by him was often regarded as an achievement of note

All of this, along with a perceived gangster connection (Toots was supposed to have once run speakeasies for Lucky Luciano), made it irresistible to a young Sinatra, and he drank there from the early 1940s onwards.

On election night, November 1944, Sinatra was drinking with a small crowd when the news of Roosevelt's victory came through. Orson Welles and Toots decided to celebrate by throwing Sinatra in the air. As an ardent Democrat he could hardly complain – besides, doing so would have been to little avail considering the relative size of his two drinking buddies.

In the early days his most likely drinking companion was Jackie Gleason, and Toots conferred on the pair the title 'crumb bums' – a sign of true affection. Sinatra and Gleason loved to needle Toots in turn. One of their favourite antics was to plead poverty and borrow cash, which they would then immediately distribute along the bar with cries of 'Drinks on the house!' They were also fond of signing Toots's name on tabs they had run up, usually adding massive gratuities to the bill. Shor eventually took revenge on Gleason by challenging him to a drinking contest and leaving him prone on the saloon floor.

In 1959 Toots sold the lease to his place for $1.5 million, and the following year he opened up at a new location at 33 West 52nd Street. That bar was closed for non-payment of taxes in 1971. He opened another restaurant eighteen months later at 5 East 54th Street, but he never managed to recapture the magic (and starry crowds) of his original lounge. He died in reduced circumstances in 1977. Jackie Gleason's flowers at the funeral had a card that read 'Save a Table for 2.'

Any crumb bum what can't get plastered by midnight
just ain't tryin' – Toots Shor

VODKA GIMLET

1½ measures of vodka ¾ measure of lime cordial 1 slice of lime	*Mix vodka and lime cordial in a chilled mixing glass with plenty of ice, shake well and strain into a Martini glass. The lime slice can be used as a garnish or placed in the glass.*

The Gimlet was originally a cocktail of gin and lime, which, according to Raymond Chandler's Philip Marlowe in *The Long Goodbye* (1953), was simply half gin and half Rose's lime juice. Both Chandler and Marlowe were of the opinion that it was a superior alternative to the Martini.

The drink probably borrowed its name from the small handheld tool for drilling holes which was often used to tap barrels and kegs, a name that reflects the sweet-tart edge of gin and lime. Alternatively, some commentators attribute the creation of the drink to a British Royal Navy surgeon, Sir Thomas Gimlette, who was said to have introduced it on board ship to combat scurvy. By the mid-twentieth century Gimlets were a favourite in the officers' messes of the British Army.

The Gimlet can be served strained into a Cocktail glass or as a rocks cocktail, poured over ice cubes placed in an Old Fashioned glass. There are debates over ratios similar to those concerning the Martini – with recipes insisting on everything from a 1:1 to a 4:1 ratio of spirit to lime. There are also those who insist that a Gimlet must be constructed with gin, but, as with the Martini, vodka soon became a popular alternative.

The makers of the television series *Mad Men* went to a great deal of trouble to reconstruct the booths at Toots Shor's in an episode when central characters Don Draper and Roger Sterling take their wives to dinner at the famous bar. Roger takes Martinis with olives, Don Old Fashioneds and Mrs Sterling a Collins. Betty Draper, however, chooses Vodka Gimlets to accompany her lobster – a choice she later regrets. Despite the programme's scrupulous attention to detail as regards food, décor and drink Toots's was never really a place for dinner with spouses. Although women were tolerated, an unwritten law of the establishment was that it was considered bad form to bring a wife to what was essentially a boys' clubhouse. 'The best thing you could say about his food was that it was warm,' said Jackie Gleason, 'but it was where all the good guys went.'

JOE E. LEWIS

I don't trust camels or anyone else who can go two weeks without a drink.

Sinatra and friends watch Joe E. Lewis play darts, Miami, 1965

Joe E. Lewis, a beloved elder statesman in Sinatra's crowd, began his show business career as a nightclub singer, but in 1927 he made the mistake of turning down an invitation from one of Al Capone's lieutenants to perform at the Green Mill Cocktail Lounge in Chicago. Shortly afterwards he was left for dead in his hotel room with his throat slashed.

He went on to become a successful comedian and singer. Much of his humour relied on his apparent fondness for booze – 'I always wake up at the crack of ice' – but this was no affectation. He was a deeply serious drinker. As well as being a close personal friend, Sinatra also played a version of Lewis in the 1957 film *The Joker Is Wild*, which was based on Lewis's official biography.

When Sinatra set up Reprise Records he released an album by Lewis entitled *It's Post Time* – a popular call for raised glasses.

Lewis was the master of the glorious ad lib, something he demonstrated when Frank Sinatra Jr made his singing début at New York's Americana Hotel. A whole bevy of Frank senior's friends turned up to support the boy, including Toots Shor, Jackie Gleason and Lewis. It was reported in *Newsweek* that Gleason was 'so overcome he had to cry a little'. When Frank junior sang 'Someday My Happy Arms Will Find You' so, too, did Lewis. Wiping away the tears he explained, 'He's talking about a bottle of Scotch.'

It was not unknown for Sinatra and Lewis to disappear off together on drinking sprees, and during one such they found themselves, for no particular reason they could recall, in Paris. Since neither of them spoke French, communicating with the locals was problematic. One afternoon Lewis came staggering into Sinatra's room with some exciting news.

'I finally met someone who speaks English,' he announced.

'Who?' asked Sinatra.

'A cat. It said "Meow".'

Sinatra sharing Martinis with Jill St John, his co-star in *Tony Rome*, 1967

'Tini Time

T he 'hard white', the 'see through', the 'cold and stiff' served in the 'up glass': gin and vermouth, the Martini. The Martini has an undeniably iconic status. It is a timeless symbol of things suave and fabulous, and to lift that distinctive long-stemmed glass is to signal kinship with the glamorous urban sophisticates of the Jazz Age, members of the jet set and other twentieth-century swingers. The Martini is the cocktail-drinkers' cocktail, and very few other drinks have inspired such volumes of debate, are surrounded by such a tangle of ritual or have earned such devotion.

'Martini', said actress Clara Bow, 'is a longer word for joy', and another of its attributes is the ability to provoke lyricism among writers and other cultural figures – Ogden Nash and Dorothy Parker both composed light-hearted odes to the Martini, while E.B. White dubbed it 'the elixir of quietude', H.L. Mencken claimed it was 'as perfect as a sonnet' and Bernard DeVoto proudly hailed it as 'the supreme American gift to world culture'. Devoto also pointed out that 'you can no more keep a Martini in a refrigerator than you can keep a kiss there'.

Sinatra liked his Martinis and respected certain traditions. He regarded them as aperitifs, to be served cold and dry before a meal in order to help stimulate appetite. On some film sets he liked to invite favoured co-stars to his trailer at the end of a day's shooting to join him for what he called ''tini time'. He would don a white apron and carefully prepare the drinks himself. Bottles and Cocktail glasses were kept in his icebox; he garnished each drink with two olives on a toothpick, and if guests wanted a second – which they usually did – he would always use a fresh, cold glass.

He ignored other traditions that did not appeal to him. He sometimes preferred vodka to gin (something that might upset the purists who insist a Martini can only ever be a gin-based drink), and the whole debate about stirring or shaking did not interest him; he would take it either way as long as it was properly chilled. His old drinking buddy Jackie Gleason always ordered his Martinis with a single olive but never ate them. He would line them up along the bar as markers so he never lost count. Sinatra usually only consumed one of his two olives; the other would be offered to a fellow drinker as a sign of friendship.

When he first auditioned for the role of Maggio in *From Here to Eternity* he acted out a couple of key scenes for the screen test. The most important of these was a bar scene, and director Fred Zimmerman asked Sinatra to improvise. He picked up two olives, rolled them along the bar like imaginary craps dice and exclaimed, *Aw, snake eyes! That's the story of my life*. He liked to believe it was that performance that earned him his comeback role, and he would reprise it for friends on a regular basis.

For his classic Dry he liked Beefeater, a premium dry gin from London that had been introduced to the American market shortly after the Second World War and quickly became one of the top import brands. If he decided to sip a vodka Martini instead his choice would be Stolichnaya or Absolut. In either case they needed to be very dry (only a splash of vermouth) and very, very cold.

THE MARTINI

A Potted History

Recipes for gin cocktails and fancy gin cocktails were popular as early as the mid-nineteenth century and were usually sweet drinks. The term 'Martini' was first used in Harry Johnson's *New and Improved Illustrated Bartender's Manual (or How to Mix Drinks of the Present Style)*, published in 1882. Johnson's recipe called for equal measures of sweet vermouth and gin, dashes of bitters and gomme syrup. Professor Jerry Thomas (not an actual professor but a major celebrity barman of his day) included a drink he named 'Martinez' in the 1887 edition of his *Bartender's Guide and Bon Vivant's Companion*, but this was another sweet gin drink laced with gomme syrup and curaçao. The first recipe that called for both dry gin and vermouth appeared in Thomas Stuart's 1896 *Fancy Drinks and How to Mix Them*; Stuart, however, christened his drink the 'Marguerite'.

By 1900 the Dry Martini was replacing sweet as the standard version of the drink. It was the appropriately named Martini di Taggio di Arma, head bartender at the Knickerbocker Hotel in New York, who helped popularize this new trend. His speciality was a carefully prepared mixture of dry gin and dry vermouth with a dash of orange bitters, stirred with ice and strained into a chilled Cocktail glass. Customers such as John D. Rockefeller would order the drink by asking for 'one of Martini's Drys'. Other bars soon followed suit. A Manhattan barman by the name of Robert Agneau first added a pitted olive as garnish, and other refinements included lemon zest, squeezed and then placed on the surface.

It was in the 1920s that the Martini began to be more or less exclusively presented in the classic Cocktail glass with the straight-edged bowl and often referred to as the 'up glass'. This distinctive glass soon became an integral part of the drink's identity – not only is it aesthetically pleasing but it has practical qualities, as the wide-lipped rim ensures that the contents are consumed properly (never gulped but sipped steadily), while the stem allows the drink to be held by the neck, keeping warmth from the hand away from the bowl. The 1920s was also the era of Prohibition in the Martini's homeland, although this did little to inhibit the drinking of cocktails. In fact, the opposite was true. Before Prohibition most of the alcohol drunk in America had been beer, but bootleggers soon realized that spirits were easier to transport and had a much higher profit margin. Cocktails flourished and became ever more elaborate, with decorations and flavourings designed to mask the taste of suspect base spirits.

The Martini received presidential backing when Roosevelt mixed up a batch in front of cameras at the White House to celebrate the repeal of

Prohibition. The President was particularly fond of a Dirty Martini – a Dry with an added dash of olive brine. By now the Dry had a ratio of at least 2:1 in favour of gin. Throughout the 1930s and 1940s the Martini made further inroads into the mainstream and was sipped onscreen by Myrna Loy and William Powell in the hugely popular *Thin Man* films; it travelled abroad and became fashionable throughout Europe.

The Second World War dampened spirits, but in 1944 Ernest Hemingway and a group of soldiers celebrated the liberation of Paris by placing an order for seventy-three Martinis at the Hotel Ritz. When the Allied leaders met to discuss their defeat of the Axis Powers Churchill happily accepted a celebratory Martini from Roosevelt, although Stalin complained that the drink was cold on the stomach. (Some years later Khrushchev declared it to be the USA's most lethal weapon.)

Having survived Prohibition, the Depression and two world wars, the Martini became a luminous, sparkling emblem of America's emerging prosperity and was used to toast an unprecedented era of technological advance, expanding affluence and superpower status. The 1950s was the golden age of the Martini. In 1952 the *New York Times* tutted that the cult of the Dry Martini might well earn the decade the name 'the Glazed Fifties'. The three-Martini lunch became *de rigueur* for young company men, and at social gatherings a successfully prepared Dry was considered an accomplishment and marker of status. Dry by now commonly meant a ratio of at least 3:1. By the 1960s the common ratio was 4:1 minimum. Perfectionists could purchase a MartiniMatic, a device that could be programmed to deliver your preferred measures of gin and vermouth automatically.

In 1966 the American Standards Association listed a recipe for the Standard American Dry Martini in their annual report, but by then the traditional Martini had a serious rival. The first recipe for a Vodkatini had appeared in Ted Saucier's 1951 cocktail book *Bottoms Up*, and this new vogue spread rapidly. The popularity of vodka in the West began in the late 1940s with the help of the Moscow Mule. The invention of the screwdriver further boosted sales, as did the revival of the Bloody Mary. Although there were many who insisted, quite understandably, that the

Martini was a *gin* cocktail, the rise of the vodka Martini was almost inevitable, thanks, in no small part, to James Bond.

The 1970s was a dismal time for cocktail drinkers. Health issues were raised, and the fashion was for mineral waters, light beers and spritzers. Jimmy Carter even singled out the three-Martini lunch as a prime example of excessive corporate greed. There was a cocktail revival of sorts in the 1980s, but it favoured drinks such as the Piña Colada, gaudy concoctions that relied on much crushed ice, fruit, paper umbrellas and novelty straws.

The Martini did, however, return to the forefront in the 1990s when cocktail culture was embraced by a whole new generation. A subculture that fashioned itself as 'lounge' sprang up through websites and retro-chic clubs. Capitol, Sinatra's old label, released a Grammy Award-winning series of *Ultra Lounge* compilations (Frank himself was noticeable by his absence, but Dean and Sammy were represented), an online manifesto was launched, *Cocktail Nation*, and magazines such as *Esquire* and *Allure* featured articles on the new fashion ('Martinis are a must,' insisted *Allure*). Much of the flavour of the movement was captured by the 1996 film *Swingers*, which featured Martini-sipping leads who based their style, attitude and jargon on Vegas-era Sinatra and Martin.

For purists, however, this revival was a mixed blessing. The Dry was supposedly back in favour, but it had to compete with all manner of new Martini hybrids. Even those who allowed that a Martini might be mixed with vodka might have baulked at the Mezcatini (mescal and vodka), the Tequini (tequila and vodka) or the Double-Chocolate Martini, and these were merely the tip of a scent-infused, liqueur-flavoured, edible-flower-garnished iceberg.

Some hybrids are still with us, although many of the more ludicrous have happily faded away, and thanks to the influence of *Mad Men*, and regular announcements from the drinks industry about the return of the classic cocktail, the Dry as it was properly conceived – an ice-cold mix of dry vermouth, strong gin, served in an up glass and garnished with a green olive – is once again being consumed.

What follows are notes on the correct construction and presentation of the Dry Martini with emphasis on what Sinatra might call 'the particulars'.

DRY MARTINI

4 measures of dry gin
1 measure of dry vermouth
1 pitted green olive

Deceptively simple ingredients, but there are several points to consider:

The Gin – Gin was originally a Dutch drink, and until the late nineteenth century other countries that produced it copied the Dutch style, which was pungent, heavily flavoured with juniper and sweetened. By the end of the nineteenth century a much more subtle and less saccharine style of gin was becoming fashionable, and the adjective 'dry' used to distinguish it from traditional gin. London eventually became a centre for gin distilling, and the appellation 'dry London gin' became universal for the new style. A Dry Martini should be prepared with a premium London dry-style gin.

The Vermouth – Vermouth is a fortified wine flavoured with herbs and plant extracts, first produced in eighteenth-century Piedmont, a region of Italy rich in both wine and herbs. The dominant style was *rosso*, based on red wine and sweetened with caramel. In the early nineteenth century the French began producing a much less sweetened, pale vermouth from white wine. This style became known as 'dry'. A Dry Martini is made with dry vermouth.

The Ratio – The ratio of gin to vermouth determines the dryness of a Martini. The earliest versions of Martini used equal measures of sweet gin and *rosso* vermouth. By the early twentieth century dry gin and dry vermouth were being employed, but the ratios remained the same. The 1930 edition of *The Savoy Cocktail Book* still recommended about half gin and half vermouth for its Martini, but after the Second World War dry started to mean more gin and less vermouth. A post-war Dry Martini would begin with a ratio of about 3:1, and throughout the 1950s and 1960s ratios of 4:1, 6:1 or even 8:1 were not uncommon. There were several noted drinkers who preferred their Martinis even drier. Ernest Hemingway had a 15:1 mixture he called the 'Montgomery', claiming that was the ratio of British troops to German that British general Monty favoured before he attacked. The Queen Mother was thought to prefer 11:1, and Winston Churchill liked to drink stone-cold gin 'while glancing at a bottle of vermouth'.

Ice – The Martini is a chilled drink, mixed with ice and strained before serving. It should be mixed with cubed ice because crushed or cracked ice will melt faster and may dilute the liquor. Even better if the cubes are of mature ice – that is, ice that has sat undisturbed in a freezer for a minimum of 48 hours, which takes even longer to melt. There should *never* be in any ice present in the finished drink. It is also essential to keep bottles in the freezer or refrigerator and to ensure that both mixing glass and Cocktail glasses are kept chilled.

Mixing – If we accept that any ratio above 4:1 is a matter of personal taste and ignore arguments over whether a true Martini is only ever a gin cocktail, then the next great controversy is concerned with mixing the drink. Traditionalists will insist that the Dry Martini should only ever be stirred and never shaken. The two main reasons for this are:

(1) violent shaking may dislodge flecks of ice, which may pass through a strainer and float in the drink;

(2) shaking produces tiny air bubbles, and aerated gin takes on a cloudy, greyish hue; this is known as 'bruising'.

Although the clouding is a temporary effect, a Dry Martini should be served clear and cold. There is also some evidence that shaking may oxidize molecules called aldehydes, and this may slightly alter the taste.

Although mixing may be done in a standard cocktail shaker, this may impart a slight metallic taste to the liquid. For this reason many purists prefer to use a mixing glass or pitcher together with a cocktail strainer. The glass, pitcher or shaker should be half-filled with ice; gin and vermouth are then poured over the ice.

Stirring is best done with a glass rod rather than a long-handled bar spoon (which may impart a metallic taste) and should be brisk but not violent. The drink should be stirred for a minimum of fifteen seconds, roughly twenty revolutions, then poured immediately into a fresh glass. (Although not essential, the stirrer may employ a look of amused *ennui* while engaged in the task.)

Dry Martinis should always be constructed as required and never mixed in batches or prepared in advance. Any excess should be poured away and the shaker or mixing glass rinsed and thoroughly dried after each drink. They must be served in the traditional up glass.

A single pitted green olive is the traditional garnish. Many cocktail olives come stuffed with pimento or even lemon paste and may be used according to taste. Olives may be discarded or consumed. It is also acceptable to drop a squeeze of lemon zest on to the surface of the drink.

Remember: One is necessary; two are dangerous, three are not enough.

FLAME OF LOVE MARTINI

1 measure of La Ina
sherry
4 measures of vodka
2 strips of orange
peel
1 book of matches

Pour the sherry into a chilled, stemmed Martini glass, swirl several times and then discard. Squeeze the first orange strip into the glass then flambé it with a match. Throw away the peel and fill the glass with ice, when it is chilled again discard the ice. Add very cold vodka then flambé the second strip of orange peel around the rim. Throw out the burnt peel, stir gently and serve.

The flame was a legendary Martini served at Chasen's restaurant, Beverley Hills, where it was created by head bartender Pepe Ruiz. In the 1960s Dean Martin was a regular, and one night he complained to Pepe that he was becoming bored with his usual Dry Martini. Pepe sensed a challenge and spent the next few weeks experimenting in private before perfecting his new Smoked Martini. When he finally presented Dean with his bespoke flame of love, Dean approved wholeheartedly.

When Sinatra was introduced to the flame he loved it, too – so much so that at one party at Chasen's he placed an order for sixty-five flames for his guests. The restaurant came close to burning down that night.

THE VESPER

1 measure of
Gordon's gin
1 measure of vodka
½ measure of Kina
Lillet Blanc
1 thin slice of lemon
peel

Pour the gin and Kina Lillet into a cocktail shaker half filled with ice and shake very well until very cold. Strain into a chilled, deep champagne goblet, add the lemon peel and serve.

The first James Bond novel, *Casino Royale*, appeared in 1952 and became an international bestseller. Ian Fleming was a former British Intelligence

Officer, and he gave his fictional spy many of his own personal tastes. Fleming was a great vodka drinker and despised Martinis mixed from bathtub gin and sherry. In *Casino Royale* Bond instructs a barman how to mix this vodka Martini. It was Fleming's own recipe, and it is named in honour of the book's female heroine, Vesper Lynd.

This particular medium-dry vodka Martini managed to break most of the etiquette concerning the classic Martini, mixing, as it does, gin and vodka with Kina Lillet Blanc, a French aperitif similar to vermouth. Bond also stipulated that it be shaken not stirred in order to deliberately achieve a misty effect. By the 1960s Bond was becoming an established screen icon and helped make vodka Martinis popular by continuing to sip them throughout the franchise.

During the Cold War a certain US Intelligence Agency experimented for a time with the idea of making the Martini a surveillance device. They created a fake olive containing a transmitter and housed a copper-wire antenna in a toothpick. The device could be left in a drained Martini glass without arousing suspicion, but the addition of any liquid would cause it to short-circuit, so it was abandoned.

LAYAWAY

4 measures of dry gin 1 measure of green chartreuse 1 lemon twist	*Pour the green chartreuse into a chilled Martini glass, swirl several times until coated, then discard liquid. Add ice-cold gin that has been stirred in the traditional Dry manner. Garnish with the lemon twist and serve.*

There are recipes for ultra-Dry Martinis that call for vermouth merely to coat the glass before gin is added; this variation on the theme was a particular fancy of F. Scott Fitzgerald, author of Sinatra's favourite book, *The Great Gatsby*. Fitzgerald was a notorious drinker, so much so that one of his friends insisted that 'before he buys a tie he has to ask if gin will make it run'. For a time he and his wife Zelda were part of a crowd of literary expats who occasionally frequented Harry's New York Bar in Paris and enjoyed traditional breakfast Martinis mixed using Noilly Prat.

Concerns about his excessive consumption once led the American humorist Robert Benchley to enquire, 'Don't you know drinking's a slow death?'

Fitzgerald's reply was 'I'm in no hurry.'

GIBSON (1)

4 measures of gin 1 measure of dry vermouth 1 cocktail (pearl) onion	*Fill a mixing glass with cracked ice, pour over the gin then the vermouth. Stir in a leisurely fashion until properly cold, strain into a chilled Martini glass and garnish with the onion skewered on a cocktail stick.*

The Gibson in this case is in almost every way actually a standard Dry, the only difference being the garnish. As usual with bar lore there is more than one version of the events leading to this innovation. The most oft-repeated tale involves the American artist Charles Dana Gibson – who achieved fame with his illustrations of the 'Gibson Girl' – challenging Charlie Conway, head barman at the Players Club in New York, to improve on his regular Dry. The response was to present the drink with an onion rather than a green olive. Presumably Gibson approved of the move, since the result was then named in his honour.

It has also been claimed that the original Gibson was in fact a Prohibition-era American diplomat on a European posting. This Gibson was teetotal, and to avoid any embarrassment or misunderstandings at the many functions he was obliged to attend he would ask bar staff to supply him with a Martini glass filled with water. The onion was added to ensure he would never inadvertently drink from a glass containing actual gin.

In a similar story Gibson is a businessman who survives countless three-Martini lunches (and steals a march on his befuddled rivals) by inventing his own unique Martini which is actually just water with an onion marker.

There is apparently another tale involving twin sisters from Chicago called Gibson, but details are scanty . . .

GIBSON (2)

2 measures of gin 2 measures of dry vermouth 1 maraschino cherry	*Fill a mixing glass or shaker with cracked ice.* *Pour over the gin and vermouth, stir until cold,* *strain into chilled Cocktail glass and present* *with the cherry.*

Although the majority of customers and many bartenders know the Gibson as a Dry with an onion, there is another version of the drink that some claim as the original. This Gibson is comparatively vermouth-heavy and features neither onion nor olive – employing instead a maraschino cherry. A recipe for this Gibson appeared in Patrick Duffy's 1934 book *The Official Mixer's Manual.*

VODKATINI

4 measures of vodka 1 measure of dry vermouth 1 lemon twist	*Pour the vodka and vermouth into a chilled* *shaker filled with ice. Shake well and pour into* *a chilled Martini glass. Garnish with a single* *lemon twist.*

Purists will argue, and it is difficult to fault their logic, that there is no such thing as a vodka Martini since the Martini is by definition a gin cocktail. The hybrid term 'Vodkatini' is commonly in use for this drink, which was originally known as the 'Kangaroo' (the origin of which name is obscure). The rise of vodka coincided with a post-Second World War shortage of traditional aged whiskies. This Russian or Polish import was virtually unknown before the war. In 1950 40,000 cases were sold in the USA, but by 1955 it was 4 million. By the mid-1960s it was outselling gin, and by 1976 it outsold whiskey. In the Martini renaissance of the late 1980s and early 1990s vodka supplanted gin as the most popular base spirit for 'up drinks'.

As well as the most obvious difference there are some more subtle variations between the Vodkatini and the more traditional Dry. It is, apparently, more than acceptable to prepare a Vodkatini by shaking it. It is thought to achieve coldness more rapidly this way, and bruising is not a consideration. It is also most commonly presented *sans* olive with only a single lemon twist.

Sinatra was not overly fond of gin but had a great fondness for good vodka. Cold vodka. Warm vodka ranked alongside the smell of roasting lamb as one of his pet hates.

P.J. CLARKE'S

'We walked into P.J. Clarke's. I said, "Vinny, my usual," and he lined up six double vodkas.' – Richard Harris.

The *New York Times* has described P.J. Clarke's as 'the Vatican of saloons'. A traditional burnished-wood tavern, it was an unlikely hang-out for celebrities, but, as well as Richard Harris, the clientele has included other dedicated drinkers such as Peter O'Toole and stars such as Marilyn Monroe, Tony Bennett, Nat King Cole, Sarah Vaughan, Johnny Mathis, Johnny Carson and Woody Allen. It was where Jacqueline Kennedy brought her children to lunch on Saturdays, the place where Buddy Holly proposed to his wife.

It was originally opened in 1884, in a building on the corner of Third Avenue and East 55th Street in Manhattan owned by a Mr Duneen. Around 1912 the bar was taken over by Patrick J. Clarke, a former employee, who changed the name and lived above the saloon from 1916 to 1937. Clarke died in 1948, and ownership was eventually purchased by the Lavezzos, antique dealers who were already tenants in the same building and who had been regular patrons of the bar. They resisted attempts to buy them out in the late 1960s, resulting in a forty-seven-storey skyscraper being built around the humble tavern.

Officially a restaurant as well as a bar, it became famous throughout the city for its simple fare. Nat King Cole famously insisted that P.J. Clarke's bacon cheeseburger was the Cadillac of cheeseburgers. There were even more ardent fans. Throughout the 1950s one customer regularly visited with his Great Dane. The dog would routinely eat at least thirty burgers at a sitting and was given a discount, since he did not require burger buns.

P.J. Clarke's was the model for Nat's Bar in the classic film *The Lost Weekend*. The author of the book on which the film was based, Charles R. Jackson, had been a regular at Clarke's.

More recently several characters from *Mad Men* made Clarke's
a regular hang-out.

It was for many years a favourite spot for Sinatra to end an
evening in the city, but it has an even more important place in
Frank lore. Legend has it that Johnny Mercer wrote the lyrics for
'One for My Baby' on a napkin there.

SIDECAR

| 1½ measures of brandy
¾ measure of Cointreau
¾ measure of fresh lemon juice | *Combine all ingredients in a shaker filled with cracked ice. Shake energetically and strain into a chilled cocktail glass.* |

If one measure of a cocktail's eminence and pedigree is the
number of competing legends concerning its origins, then the
Sidecar certainly deserves serious consideration as a contender
to be listed among the classics. The most common explanation
for the name is that it was the favourite drink of an army officer
(possibly retired, probably British) who drank it at the Ritz (or
sometimes Harry's Bar) in Paris. The gentleman in question
always arrived in a chauffeur-driven motorcycle sidecar. Some
books claim the cocktail was invented during the First World
War; others that it was first created by Harry MacElhone (of the
original Harry's Bar) in 1931. There is, however, a version of the
drink in the 1930 edition of Harry Craddock's *Savoy Cocktail
Book*. The Harry MacElhone version stipulated equal measures
of Cointreau, cognac and lemon juice; Craddock suggested
a 2:1 ratio of brandy (rather than cognac) to Cointreau. Who
the gentleman in the sidecar was, and where he first sipped the
drink, we may never know for certain, but this cocktail is one of
the finest sours conceived and has been one of the specialities at
P.J. Clarke's now for decades.

HUMPHREY BOGART

'I should never have switched from Scotch to Martinis.' –
Humphrey Bogart's last words (allegedly)

According to Sydney Greenstreet, while addressing Bogart's Sam Spade in *The Maltese Falcon*, you should always be suspicious of a man who, when offered a drink, says 'when'. The logic to this was that if a fellow has to be careful not to drink too much it is because he is not to be trusted when drunk. In real life Bogart had his own views on the matter of alcohol, summed up in the glorious motto: 'Never trust a bastard who doesn't drink.'

Frank Sinatra's opinion of Bogart was little short of hero worship. For a young Sinatra Bogart appeared to represent the hard-drinking, tough-talking, bruised-but-romantic loner Sinatra thought he aspired to become. Bogie was a cult hero to many in the Hollywood community – he managed to achieve star status while making clear his distaste for the ass-kissing, back-biting and hypocrisy so prevalent in the film industry. The public loved him despite (or because of) his liberal politics and his general air of non-conformity. He even had a successful marriage.

Their first meeting, however, could easily have been disastrous. It was in 1945 at the Players, the bar, restaurant and theatre owned by Preston Sturges. The press had already trumpeted Sinatra's arrival in Hollywood, and Bogart was predisposed to have a poor opinion of the bobbysoxer idol, the Sultan of Swoon, who was trying to make it big in films.

'They tell me you have a voice that makes girls faint,' sneered Bogart. 'Make me faint.'

Sinatra managed to hold his nerve and shrugged, saying, 'I'm taking the week off.'

After that the two men met occasionally between filming and recording sessions and enjoyed drinking together. When Sinatra moved his family to Holmby Hills, Los Angeles, in 1949 the new house was only blocks away from the Bogarts, and Sinatra was soon part of the drinking set that the press dubbed the 'Holmby Hills Rat Pack'.

Bogart was a man of substance and strength, but the street-smart tough-guy persona that attracted Sinatra was an invention. Bogart was actually the son of a prominent New York surgeon and had a privileged childhood, attending private school and an Ivy League college before briefly serving in the navy at the close of the First World War. He was cultured and well read, which was something else Sinatra aspired to.

Frank would have loved to be Bogart, but he rarely listened properly to the older, wiser man's advice; if he had it might have saved him a deal of grief. Bogart summed up the root of many of Frank's problems when he opined that Sinatra's idea of paradise was a place where there are plenty of women and no newspapermen – although he would be better off if it was the other way around. For his part Sinatra claimed to be genuinely perplexed that somebody of Bogart's status never seemed to take up the many opportunities offered him to sleep with women other than his wife. But then he was married to Lauren Bacall.

Bogart and Bacall were there for Sinatra when both his marriage and career were failing. Although separated from Nancy he spent many nights sleeping on her sofa and almost as many crashing out at the Bogarts across the way. 'He's always here,' Bogart told a reporter.

In 1956 Bogart was diagnosed with terminal throat cancer. He took almost a year to die, and Sinatra took every opportunity he could to visit, but in January 1957, when Bogart passed away, Sinatra was working in New York at the Copacabana. He cancelled three dates but was too upset to travel back for the funeral and holed up alone instead in his Manhattan hotel. For some time afterwards he comforted Bacall and even, apparently, proposed marriage. When news of an engagement leaked to the press he blamed Bacall and refused to speak to her for years. Guilt.

Sinatra drinking cocktails with Ava Gardner, the woman who taught him how to sing a torch song. It was an addictive and destructive passion, a doomed love affair. 'Ava loved Frank', said Hank Sanicola, 'but not the way he loved her.'

Exotic Booze

Throughout the 1950s America developed a fascination with far-flung, exotic destinations. *National Geographic* subscriptions soared, Disney offered rides such as the Jungle Cruise and Robinson Crusoe's Desert Island Hideaway and crowds flocked to lush Technicolor fantasies such as *South Pacific* and *The King and I*. An emerging musical genre that became known as 'exotica' saw the likes of Martin Denny and Les Baxter producing hit albums that took advantage of new recording techniques to use everything from temple bells and birdsong to create aural travelogues that were played on newly available and affordable domestic hi-fi systems. Food and drink were also being exoticized with rum-and-pineapple cocktails served in coconut husks in Polynesian-themed bars and restaurants, including Don the Beachcomber and Trader Vic's.

Sinatra never attempted to record exotica, but as a renowned international playboy and fully fledged jet-setter he issued an invitation to join him in his wanderings with the 1958 release of the album *Come Fly with Me*. The album's title track and closing song – 'It's Nice to Go Trav'ling' – were specific commissions, written by Sammy Cahn and Jimmy Van Heusen. Cahn originally penned the famous line about 'exotic booze' and bars in far Bombay but decided to censor himself and substitute the word 'views' in place of 'booze'. The track was recorded with the more family-orientated line, but when Cahn mentioned in passing the change he had made Sinatra recalled all the musicians and did it again with the more appropriate word back in its rightful place. The album was Sinatra's first collaboration with arranger-composer Billy May, another legendary boozer who often began recording sessions by warning musicians that there would be no drinking *off* the job. To reinforce the message and set an example he would sometimes count in tempo using a fifth of overproof vodka, taking large swigs on the beat. He had a reputation among his peers as a man who could conduct a full chorus and orchestra while stone drunk. His antics had Sinatra rolling on the floor. When the single 'Come Fly with Me' was released in 1957 it went straight to number one in the Billboard pop charts.

MAI TAI

2 measures of Wray and Nephew seventeen-year-old rum
½ measure of triple sec
¼ measure of orgeat (almond syrup)
¼ measure of sugar syrup
Juice of one large lime
Sprig of mint

Combine ingredients in a shaker with one glassful of crushed ice, shake well and strain into a Cocktail glass. Add half the spent lime shell and garnish with the mint.

It was Victor Bergeron, founder of Trader Vic's, who created the first Mai Tai. Some time around 1944 he was visited by two Tahitian friends, and to celebrate their arrival he decided to concoct a special drink. With the help of the head barman at his restaurant of the time – Hinky Dink's in Emeryville, California – he selected what he considered to be the finest ingredients and combined them in the manner described above. When his thirsty guests tasted their new cocktail they praised it as *mai tai-roa aé*, which Vic claimed translated as 'the best thing we've ever drunk'.

By the 1950s Trader Vic's restaurants were booming, and Bergeron decided to make the Mai Tai available to his customers. They were so popular that the world's entire supply of seventeen-year-old rum was soon depleted, so the recipe for the signature cocktail was amended, the precious Wray and Nephew rum replaced by one measure each of more ordinary white and dark rum.

DAIQUIRI

2 measures of white rum
1 dash of maraschino liqueur
Juice of one medium lime
1 tablespoon of caster sugar

Dissolve the sugar in lime juice in a cocktail shaker. Add the rum and crushed ice and shake rapidly until very cold. Strain into a frosted champagne or Martini glass.

Although the Daiquiri's origins are obviously Cuban, it is claimed that the original recipe is held at the Army and Navy Club in Washington, DC. It was said to have been invented by an American engineer, Jennings Cox, who ran out of gin while working at a mine near the town of Daiquiri, Santiago, Cuba, and improvised a drink from local ingredients. It was brought from Cuba to the USA by Admiral Lucas Johnson in 1909 and became so popular that the club installed a brass plaque in its Daiquiri Lounge celebrating Johnson's achievement.

The Daiquiri's most glorious period was during Prohibition, when thirsty Americans made drinking jaunts to Cuba. The drink put in an appearance in F. Scott Fitzgerald's *This Side of Paradise*, and other celebrity imbibers included Hemingway, who liked his doubled, and Marlene Dietrich, who sipped hers in the Savoy's American Bar in London. Constantino Ribailagua, barman at Havana's famous El Floridita Bar, mixed and strained his Daiquiris so expertly that customers never encountered any sliver of ice in the finished cocktail. As with the Martini, the classic Daiquiri should be served ice cold but completely undiluted. Again, as with Martini, there is some debate concerning particulars such as the garnish. Purists insist that none is necessary, while others allow for a twist of lime peel or a cherry, the latter complementing the maraschino liqueur, which is made from cherries.

Frozen Daiquiris are an accepted variation for many, usually achieved by placing all the ingredients (including ice) in a blender and pouring without straining. Sloppy Joe's bar in Havana was renowned for both standard and Frozen Daiquiris, and Hemingway wrote that drinking them made you feel like you were skiing downhill through powder snow.

More controversial are fruit Daiquiris – the most popular being banana and strawberry – which are created using fruit syrup or liqueur and quantities of ripe fruit. For traditionalists sweetness in a Daiquiri is something to be avoided. According to Charles Baker in *The Gentleman's Companion*: 'A too-sweet Daiquiri is like a lovely lady with too much perfume.'

FLORIDITA SPECIAL

4 measures of rum
2 level teaspoons of granulated sugar
2 teaspoons of grapefruit juice
2 teaspoons of maraschino liqueur
Juice of one medium lime
3 cups of finely cracked ice

All ingredients should be added to a blender then blitzed at high speed for twenty seconds before being poured into a chilled Cocktail glass.

The secret to re-creating the authentic Floridita Frozen Daiquiri is two-fold. First, all the ingredients must be added to the blender glass in the order listed. Second, the drink should be watched carefully while it blends. Twenty seconds is a guide time, judging by eye the point at which the drink reaches perfection and achieves the consistency of lightly frozen sherbet but without any significant pieces of ice.

MOJITO

2½ measures of white or
golden rum
Juice of half a lime
3–4 sprigs of fresh mint
⅔ measure of sugar
syrup
1 dash of Angostura
bitters
Soda water

Place the mint leaves in the bottom of a Collins glass and crush. Add shaved ice and the spent lime shell. Shake the rum, lime juice, bitters and syrup together and strain into the glass. Top up with soda water and serve with straws.

Of the three most famous Havana bars frequented by visiting Americans – Sloppy Joe's, El Floridita and La Bodeguita del Medio – La Bodeguita was Hemingway's favourite, chiefly because the management extended him credit. It was here, during the 1920s, that the traditional recipe for Mojito was revived with great success, going on to become a cocktail of international renown and popularity.

Cuba in the 1920s and 1930s was a romantic playground for literary ex-pats and American tourists eager to escape the stifling restrictions of Prohibition. In 1940 Fulgencio Batista staged a coup and took power, and he was more than happy to exploit the potential for corruption, and the country's legal gambling and lax extradition laws attracted a far less salubrious class of visitor. In 1947 Sinatra was photographed arriving in Havana, walking down the steps of a Pan Am clipper in the company of two known mobsters. Sinatra and one of the men both had attaché cases, which federal investigators strongly suspected contained two million dollars – tribute being paid to the exiled Mob boss Lucky Luciano. It sparked early rumours of gangster affiliations that would plague Sinatra for most of his career.

CUBA LIBRE

3 measures of white or golden rum
1 small lime
Coca-Cola

Pour the rum into a Highball glass filled with ice. Cut the lime into quarters and squeeze into the glass. Add cola, stir and present.

'*¡Cuba Libre!*' (Free Cuba) was the battle cry of the Cuban Liberation Army. Cuba was freed from Spanish rule in 1898 following the Spanish-American War, and Cubans toasted the American forces that had helped them achieve freedom with this classic Highball. Since Coca-Cola was not available in Cuba until after 1900 the original drink used a dark, sweet syrup made from kola nuts and coca. Returning troops helped popularize the drink throughout the USA.

After marrying in secret in Pennsylvania in November 1951 Sinatra and Ava Gardner flew to Havana, the birthplace of the Cuba Libre, for a brief and ecstatic honeymoon. They spent their time drinking Cuba Libres in nightclubs and dancing until daybreak. Such good times could not last, and the arguments began soon after they returned home.

BLUE HAWAII

1½ measures of white rum
1½ measures of dark rum
½ measure of blue curaçao
3 measures of pineapple juice
1 measure of coconut cream

Blend all the ingredients with a small cup of crushed ice. Pour into a goblet, garnish with a pineapple slice and present with short straws.

Hawaii had been drawn into the economic network of the USA from the end of the nineteenth century onwards, and the Hawaiian Islands were a source of fascination for many suburban Americans. After it became the fiftieth state of the union in 1959 it rivalled Las Vegas as the coolest vacation spot inside the USA. Sinatra recorded 'Blue Hawaii' for *Come Fly with Me* four years before Elvis Presley played Chad Gates, the son of a pineapple tycoon, in the film of the same name.

Sinatra had spent time in Hawaii in 1953 filming outdoor scenes for *From Here to Eternity*. He was extremely grateful to be playing what he considered the role of a lifetime, the grinning, boozing, tough little Italian-American GI Angelo Maggio whose refusal to be broken ends in tragedy. The film would mark the start of his comeback, but off screen his personal life was fraught. His marriage to Ava was barely a year old and in trouble. She was in Nairobi filming *Mogambo*, and telephone connections between East Africa and Hawaii were precarious. When he did manage to get through Ava was often unavailable. He consoled himself by drinking heavily, mostly with co-star Montgomery Clift, who shared a hatred of being alone and had his own problems. Clift's capacity for booze was limited, and Burt Lancaster usually ended up putting both men to bed.

Sinatra had a happier time in Hawaii in 1961 while filming *The Devil at 4 o'Clock*. He spent much of his free time arranging *luau* benefits for the Kennedy campaign, performing with local musicians and drumming up support all over the islands. According to Peter Lawford, 'Frank and I won Honolulu for Jack.'

Although he loved the place and occasionally vacationed there, it must have sometimes felt to him as though he had offended the local gods. In May 1964 he came very close to drowning on a Hawaiian beach, eventually being pulled from the surf by the actor Brad Dexter. Sinatra played down the incident, claiming only that 'I got a little water on my bird.'

MARGARITA

1½ measures of gold
(oro) tequila
½ measure of triple sec
or Cointreau
Juice of one large lime
1 lime wedge
Fine salt

Rub the rim of a chilled Margarita glass with the lime wedge and then dip in the rim in a saucer of fine salt until coated. Mix the tequila, triple sec and lime juice in a shaker with cracked ice until well chilled. Strain into the salted glass and garnish with the lime wedge.

A Margarita may be served straight up if sufficiently chilled or on the rocks. Frozen Margaritas, blended with ice, became popular in the 1970s.

There are several competing legends about the origin of this cocktail, usually involving the drink being concocted in a Mexican *cantina* in honour of an esteemed female customer – variously the daughter of a diplomat, a Ziegfeld dancer or former silent movie star – some time in the 1930s or 1940s.

It has also been claimed that it was created in 1948 by Santos Cruz, chief barman at the Balinese Room in Galveston, Texas, for the singer Peggy Lee – Margarita being the Spanish equivalent of her given name, Margaret. It had, however, already been popularized in 1947 by Albert Hernández at La Plaza restaurant in La Jolla, San Diego.

Sinatra was fond of tequila. Bono from the band U2, who duetted with Sinatra on a version of 'I've Got You Under My Skin', recalled being floored by an evening's drinking with Frank that included Jack Daniel's served in a pint glass and tequila presented in a goblet the size of a goldfish bowl.

Sinatra was also fond of Mexico. In 1951, after his separation from Nancy had been made public, he flew to Acapulco with Ava. The couple were constantly harassed by the press who speculated that Sinatra was planning a quickie Mexican divorce in order to marry Ava. He wasn't. They just wanted time away together, but the vacation had to be abandoned after a few days. Sinatra was so angry that on his return home he drove his car into a pack of reporters waiting at Los Angeles Airport. Nobody was seriously hurt, but he was forced to apologize. Years later there was an actual Mexican divorce – in Ciudad Juárez – following the breakdown of his marriage to Mia Farrow.

CAIPIRINHA

2 measures of cachaça
1 small lime
1½ teaspoons of caster sugar

Top, tail and then quarter the lime lengthways and place segments skin side down in an Old Fashioned glass. Add sugar and then crush and muddle the lime until the sugar is dissolved. Fill the glass almost to the top with broken ice, pour over cachaça and stir.

Cachaça is a traditional full-strength Brazilian spirit distilled from fermented sugarcane sap, somewhere between a sugarcane brandy and unmatured white rum. Caipirinha translates as 'peasant's drink' and was a staple of the Brazilian working-man's diet, ubiquitous in small bars and cafés. Visiting Americans loved it and took the recipe home where it became a popular cocktail.

Brazilian sounds such as samba and bossa nova were wafting over the USA in the late 1950s and early 1960s. The West Coast cool-jazz school were particularly smitten, and musicians such as Stan Getz and Gerry Mulligan were among those to play around with the gently undulating rhythms and pulses. By 1963 even the mainstream pop singer Eydie Gormé had a hit with 'Blame It on the Bossa Nova'.

Antônio Carlos Jobim had started out as a piano player in the 1930s and had hung around with the *sambistas*, bohemian musicians who jammed in bars. He learned guitar from them and developed the style called 'bossa nova', which translated as 'new flair' or 'new wave'. He first found fame in his homeland in the mid-1950s when his songs were covered by Brazilian singer-guitarist João Gilberto. When Stan Getz and Astrud Gilberto, João's wife, recorded an English-language version of his 'Girl from Ipanema' in 1964 he became known internationally. By

1967 his compositions were among the most recorded of the day, their popularity even rivalling the Beatles. Around this time Sinatra decided he would like to work with him.

BOSSA NOVA

1 measure of golden rum	*Add all the ingredients to a cocktail shaker*
1 measure of Galliano	*and blend well. Strain into a Collins glass*
½ measure of apricot brandy	*filled with cracked ice. Garnish with an*
3 measures of pineapple juice	*orange slice and serve with a straw.*
½ measure of lemon juice	
1 teaspoon of egg white	

Sinatra and Billy May had included a version of the big-band standard 'Brazil' on *Come Fly with Me*, and 'The Coffee Song' had appeared on *Ring-a-Ding-Ding!*, Sinatra's first album for his own label, Reprise, but these were hardly authentic. His collaborations with Jobim were something else entirely.

Sinatra struggled to find suitable material from the late 1960s onwards. Afraid of losing his relevance and eager to reclaim chart placings he abandoned the classics from the Great American Songbook and attempted to record more contemporary material. Unfortunately his versions of songs such as 'Mrs Robinson' or 'Don't Sleep in the Subway' were unconvincing, even vaguely embarrassing, but through Jobim he discovered a contemporary idiom that he *could* succeed with, even excel at. 'I haven't sung so soft since I had the laryngitis,' joked Sinatra in the sleeve notes, but his voice was far from weak; it was wonderfully supple. The album *Francis Albert Sinatra and Antônio Carlos Jobim* featured seven of Jobim's original compositions together with three American standards adapted to the bossa-nova idiom. It was released in 1967 and easily made the Top 20. Ten more Jobim songs were recorded in 1969, seven of which appeared on side one of the 1971 album *Sinatra and Company*.

In 1980 Sinatra performed for 175,000 people at the Maracanã Stadium in Rio de Janeiro. At the time he set a record for the largest audience ever drawn by a solo artist. It was also one of the first public occasions when his age began to show. He had begun 'Strangers in the Night' but suddenly lost the lyric. What could have been a disaster became something of a triumph. 'The whole stadium started to sing it for me,' he recalled afterwards, 'in *English*. I was touched.'

NEGRONI

1 measure of gin	*Stir the ingredients with ice in a mixing*
1 measure of Campari	*glass, strain into a Rocks glass over ice and*
1 measure of sweet vermouth	*garnish with a strip of orange peel before*
1 strip of orange peel	*presenting.*

'The bitters are excellent for your liver; the gin is bad for you. They balance each other.' So said Orson Welles in 1947 after his first Negroni.

It was in Florence in 1919 that Count Camillo Negroni first partook of the cocktail that would be named for him. On the day in question the count felt the need for something stronger than his usual Americano, and Fosco Scarselli, barman at the Caffè Casoni, where the Count drank daily, obliged him by replacing the soda with gin. If the Americano was pretty but only mildly alcoholic, the new Negroni was robust and decidedly manly. It soon joined the ranks of classic three-ingredient cocktails.

The count himself was a romantic figure, described by some as a playboy. Born in Florence in 1868 to an Italian father and English mother, he was a well-travelled adventurer. As well as spending time in London, where he may have developed a love of good gin, he also travelled America, working for a time as a rodeo cowboy and a professional gambler.

The Negroni cocktail was such a success that in 1919 the Negroni family established a distillery in Treviso and produced a ready-mixed bottled version of the drink. It was a classic Italian aperitif that Sinatra would have saluted with his traditional toast, 'Cent'anni.'

THE VILLA CAPRI

Frank Sinatra says:

Patsy's Italian food is comparable to my Mom's –
and if you don't think hers is great,
you should taste my Old Man's cooking!

So ran an advertisement in *Variety* on 3 March 1952 for Patsy D'Amore's Villa Capri Restaurant. Opened in 1950 to help introduce the residents of Los Angeles to Neapolitan delicacies such as pizza, the original Villa Capri was situated half a block from Hollywood Boulevard at 1753 McCadden Place. It was an unassuming place with red-and-white chequered tablecloths and straw-covered Chianti bottles dangling from the walls, but it soon attracted what press releases described as 'showfolk and sportsmen'.

Regular celebrity clientele included, according to *Movie Star Parade Magazine*, James Dean who, after parking in an adjacent lot, entered the premises via a back door and through the kitchen before settling in his private booth to smoke Chesterfields and sip Scotch-and-water Highballs. It was also a regular hang-out for the Holmby Hills Rat Pack.

Patsy was good to Sinatra in the lean years of the early 1950s and extended him a long line of credit, and so when Sinatra's career was well and truly back on course and the lease on the original Villa Capri at an end Sinatra agreed to be co-owner of a new, improved Villa Capri Restaurant which opened in 1957 at 6735 Yucca Street. Sinatra's booth soon became his unofficial office, an HQ from where he conducted much professional as well as social business. In 1956 Capitol Records had opened a brand-new state-of-the art recording studio just seven blocks west of Villa Capri, on Vine Street. Sinatra was the first artist to use it and would often unwind at the restaurant after recording sessions. Many of his great Capitol albums were planned there during unofficial production meetings. He would dine with Nelson Riddle and producer Voyle Gilmore, discussing the selection of songs, arrangements and session musicians late into the evening. Billy May was also a regular as were musicians and singers such as Bobby Darin and Nat King Cole, while songwriters Jimmy Van Heusen and Sammy Cahn also often ate and drank there, either for pleasure or to offer Frank a new song.

The record meetings continued into the 1970s, and after Sinatra left Capitol and set up Reprise Records artists such as Count Basie, Duke Ellington and Ella Fitzgerald were entertained at the Capri. The restaurant's proximity to other recording studios and record companies – including RCA, A&M and, later, Motown (the Hollywood office of Motown had its own booth at the Capri from 1972) – made it a hub of activity for producers, performers and executives who negotiated deals over pasta and red wine.

Theatre, radio and television personalities also congregated there. It was designed to be a celebrity hang-out and attracted more than its fair share of names, becoming a popular venue in which stars, major and minor, could hold celebratory bashes (it was the venue for the wrap party for *The Godfather*), usually in the Durante room, named in honour of another regular, Jimmy Durante. Few, if any, of these gatherings came close to matching the celestial bacchanalia that took place in December 1957, the night of Sinatra's forty-second birthday celebration. Among those who took turns to serenade, eulogize or gently rib the birthday boy were Dean Martin, Eddie Fisher, Vic Damone, Bing Crosby, Jack Benny and James Cagney. The event was privately recorded, and bootleg copies became collectors' items. The Durante Room was also the venue for meetings of an organization known as the 'Sons of Italy'. These meetings often drew the attention of FBI agents who, denied access to the restaurant, would congregate in the car park taking down licence-plate numbers.

Never shy of self-promotion, Sinatra included a nod to his new investment in a swinging version of 'The Isle of Capri' included on *Come Fly with Me*. Naturally enough, towards the end of the song he substituted 'Villa Capri' for the island; more confusingly, for those not in the know, he also included a line about a beautiful girl with a lovely meatball on her finger.

The Villa Capri closed in 1982 after twenty-five years at the top. Sadly, as with many old Hollywood landmarks, the building was eventually demolished.

AMERICANO

1 measure of Campari	*Add several ice cubes to a Highball glass. Pour in the Campari and vermouth, top up with soda, stir and present with the orange slice.*
½ measure of sweet vermouth	
Soda water	
1 slice of orange	

Sinatra's father was born in Sicily, and his mother came from Genoa. Frank was extremely proud of his Italian origins, and in a nod to his heritage he occasionally took glasses of grappa, sambuca or that other Italian classic, Campari. An alcoholic liqueur infused with herbs and fruit, Campari was first formulated by Gaspare Campari in 1860 in Novara in the north-west of Italy, and it became a popular aperitif in its home country. It has a distinctive red hue; for many years this was from added carmine, a food dye derived from crushed cochineal insects, although this is no longer an ingredient.

In the 1920s it also came to be appreciated by visitors from the USA. One reason for its popularity might have been that it was officially classified as 'bitters' – a medicinal product rather than a spirit – which meant that tourists could take bottles home and legally imbibe them during Prohibition. Impressed by their visitors' love of their drink the Italians took to calling Campari and soda 'Americano'.

MIKE ROMANOFF

'Nobody knows the truth about me, not even me.'

His Highness Prince Michael Dmitri Alexandrovich Oblensky Romanoff, nephew of the assassinated Tsar Nicholas II, led a remarkable life by anyone's standards. Born in 1890 he was schooled at Eton, Harrow and Winchester, after which he attended both Oxford and Cambridge then Sandhurst as well as Harvard, Princeton, Yale, the Sorbonne and Heidelberg. He drove a taxi for the French Army during the defence of Paris then served as a lieutenant in the British Army on the Western Front before being commissioned as a Cossack officer in the Russian Army on the Eastern Front. He had been awarded the Légion d'honneur for various acts of heroic gallantry, had personally defended the gates of the Winter Palace against rampaging Bolsheviks and endured six years in solitary confinement after killing a German nobleman in a duel.

If these adventures sounded incredible, it was because very little of it was true. Prince Mike had, apparently, attended Harvard briefly to study engineering, and he was familiar with a jail cell. Everything else was pure invention.

He was born Herschel Geguzin, the son of a dried-goods merchant who owned a small shop in Vilnius, Lithuania. His father died before he was born, and at the age of ten Herschel was sent to start a new life in the USA. He grew up in New York in a series of orphanages and reform schools, eventually moving on and finding work as a farmhand in Illinois – but he was never going to be a farmer.

In the early 1920s he was in London, where his habit of passing dud cheques brought him to the attention of the authorities, and after receiving a suspended jail sentence he was strongly encouraged to leave Britain. He re-emerged in Paris, where he secured a number of loans against the millions

Sinatra, Dean Martin and Mike Romanoff arrive in London – the 'Emperor' looks displeased with his subjects.

of pounds' worth of Russian royal jewels that he insisted were about to be shipped over from Lithuania. Returning to the USA he travelled across the country implementing a number of scams. He adopted a hybrid upper-class English accent, wore a monocle and persuaded several citizens of the Midwest that he was a relative of the Duke of Wellington. He enjoyed a successful social season in New York, attending a grand ball held by the Vanderbilts – although this was marred by his arrest in Manhattan. As well as bogus loans he also developed a sideline in fine art, convincing dealers to loan him pieces that he claimed he could sell on (for a small commission) to expatriate Russian nobility.

Naturally enough he eventually gravitated towards Hollywood. A gifted self-publicist, he was sufficiently notorious to be given his own column in the *Los Angeles Times* and gained occasional work as a historical adviser on films. He was also employed by the Clover Club, a casino on Sunset Boulevard that understood the cachet a Russian prince would add. His hosting there also allowed him the opportunity to play chess and backgammon for money – and he was expert at both games. The casino was patronized by several high-rolling Hollywood executives and stars, and he made many celebrity connections. These included David Niven – whom Mike had first encountered in New York during Prohibition when both men were liquor salesmen, selling illegal booze to speakeasies – and Humphrey Bogart, who became a chess partner and close friend. In 1939 he offered his film-star friends the unique opportunity to purchase shares in a new venture. After buying a lease on a defunct restaurant he intended to create his own fine-dining establishment. Invitations to the opening night read as follows:

> *I am commanded by His Imperial Highness*
> *Prince Michael Alexandrovich Dmitri Oblensky Romanoff*
> *to request your presence at a soiree he is giving*
> *in his own honour.*
> *Cover fifty dollars.*
> *Bring your own wine and kindly fee the waiters.*

The opening was a great success, a black-tie event attended by many Hollywood stars, despite the fact that the premises had no cooking facilities. Once a meal was ordered, and paid for in advance, it was collected from a nearby hash joint. Romanoff used the money he made to install a functioning kitchen. It was the beginning of a small Hollywood restaurant empire that made Mike as much of a celebrity as his customers.

Mike Romanoff became legendary in the movie community. George Jacobs, Sinatra's personal valet for fifteen years, called him the biggest bullshit artist in the world, but this was a large part of his appeal. Nobody seriously believed that he was the nephew of the tsar, but people enjoyed pretending to believe Mike was a genuine prince. David Niven so admired his confabulations that he dedicated a whole chapter of his autobiography *Bring On the Empty Horses* to his antics.

Sinatra loved him deeply, too. Mike had been kind to him when he first moved to Hollywood, and, along with Bogart, became for a time something of a father figure. Sinatra called him the 'Emperor'. When he was pleased the Emperor would often bestow gifts on his subjects – if Frank earned his favour he might be rewarded with the Ural Mountains, for example, although this largesse might be withdrawn later if behaviour was lacking in appropriate deference or proper etiquette. Sinatra, of course, could not resist playing tricks on Mike. One of the most elaborate and longest-running centred on the simple art of 'fixing' a friend's cigarettes – surreptitiously breaking them so they were useless when taken out the packet.

On a trip to London with Dean and Mike, Sinatra stole his cigarettes in the car on the way to the airport and fixed them. He fixed the cigarettes on the airplane and phoned ahead to the Savoy, where they were staying, to arrange for all the cigarettes in the hotel room to be fixed and the packs resealed. Frank and Dean did the same thing at every restaurant they went to, every nightclub. For the whole trip Mike was faced with stubs every time he opened his cigarettes or attempted to use his gold cigarette case. They flew back to New York, where all Mike's brand of cigarettes in Sinatra's apartment had also been fixed, then finally back to their Beverley Hills homes, where Mike was certain he could finally enjoy an untampered-with smoke. Frank and Dean were invited in for a cocktail, and Mike hurried to his bar, picked out a sealed packet and opened them to reveal once again – fragments. He turned to his wife and sighed, 'Et tu, Gloria?'

Sinatra looked after Mike in his declining years, after he had lost his restaurants and most of his friends. He was welcomed into the personal entourage and accompanied Sinatra whenever possible all over Europe and to Vegas, New York, Miami. Sinatra never really tired of his company, and after his death in 1971 he was sadly missed.

'Tea For Two'. Although Sinatra occasionally took hot tea while resting his throat, everybody knew what he preferred. 'I hate water,' he would insist. 'Even my shower's got club soda in it.'

Alcoholic Remorse

'He doesn't get hangovers, he gives them,' was the opinion of one associate, and Sinatra himself was proud of his capacity and resilience. Sammy Davis was ready to swear that he only ever saw Frank really drunk once – but, of course, there were times when, even by his own generous standards, he overindulged and suffered horribly as a result.

'I feel sorry for people who don't drink,' he would quip on stage. 'When they wake up in the morning that's the best they're gonna feel all day.'

On the mornings – or, more realistically, afternoons – when he awoke feeling unwell the flag with the Jack Daniel's insignia would be replaced with one featuring Alka Seltzer, and he was likely to call for a Ramos. The Ramos Gin Fizz was a favourite hangover cure, introduced to Sinatra by Robert Mitchum. Mitchum had called it 'Mother's Milk', and Sinatra was so grateful for the introduction that for years he sent Mitchum thank-you cards on Mothers' Day.

The Bloody Mary also played its part in recoveries. In September 1961 Sinatra was invited to the Oval Office to be thanked personally by Kennedy for his work on the presidential campaign. Dave Powers, a presidential aide, recalled Sinatra and Kennedy sipping Bloody Marys on the Truman Balcony. According to Powers Sinatra had instructed the White House *maître d'* on how to prepare his own personal recipe for the famous curative. He also set a record while staying at the Sands by placing a single order for 300 Bloody Marys.

Dean Martin's advice on avoiding hangovers was to stay drunk. Faced with the inevitable, however, he resorted to malted milk.

RAMOS GIN FIZZ

2 measures of gin
1 measure of lemon juice
¾ measure of fresh lime juice
3 drops of orange-flower water
1 egg white
1 measure of full-cream milk or light whipping cream
3 measures of soda water
1 teaspoon of fine powdered sugar

Mix all the ingredients except the soda water in a chilled metal shaker with half a glass of crushed ice. Shake vigorously for at least five minutes. Pour, unstrained, into a frosted Highball glass. Add soda water and garnish with a mint sprig and/or lime wedge. Present with a straw.

The Ramos Gin Fizz was invented in 1888 at Henrico Ramos's Imperial Cabinet Saloon in New Orleans, which was closed in 1920, a victim of Prohibition. The precise formula of the Fizz had been a closely guarded secret for over thirty years, but Henrico's brother, Charles Henry, was so enraged that the so-called 'Noble Experiment' was depriving loyal customers of their beverage that he posted a copy of the recipe on the shuttered and padlocked doors. He further distributed copies throughout the city – perhaps one of the few good things to come out of Prohibition.

A tray of Fizzes was often delivered to the steam rooms of the Sands the morning after the night before.

BLOODY MARY

1 measure of vodka
5 measures of tomato juice
½ teaspoon of lemon juice
1 dash of Worcestershire sauce
4 drops of Tabasco sauce
1 pinch of celery salt
1 twist of black pepper

Pour the vodka into a large tumbler a quarter filled with ice. Add spices then top up with tomato juice. Stir well before presenting and serve with a short stick of leafy celery.

The Bloody Mary was conceived in 1921 by Ferdinand 'Pete' Petiot, barman at legendary drinking shrine Harry's New York Bar in Paris. Tomato juice and vodka was already an established combination, but Petiot added several new spiceful touches to create a distinctive prototype. Many of the regulars at Harry's had a colourful turn of phrase, and one of them christened Petiot's creation the 'Bucket of Blood'. Pete preferred it to be known as the Bloody Mary, probably in honour of silent-movie star Mary Pickford or perhaps as a nod to the Tudor Queen infamous for butchering Protestants.

In the 1956 film *The Girl Can't Help It* gangster's moll Jayne Mansfield presents her press agent, played by Tom Ewell, with a Bloody Mary with the words, 'I think you need this . . . I made them for my father. He drank a lot – tried to forget my mother.'

DEATH IN THE AFTERNOON

1 measure of absinthe
Champagne

Pour one jigger of absinthe into a champagne glass. Add chilled champagne until it attains the proper opalescent milkiness. Drink three to five of these slowly.

The instructions on preparing this particular hangover remedy came courtesy of Ernest Hemingway and were part of his contribution to a 1935 cocktail book, *So Red the Nose*, which had recipes supplied by famous authors. Hemingway relied for a long time on a mixture of tomato juice and beer to help alleviate alcoholic remorse, but during his time in Paris developed a taste for absinthe, which led to the creation of this decadent alternative. He named it after his own 1932 non-fiction book about bullfighting. After Ava Garner had a highly public fling with a matador the subject of bullfighting was not popular with Frank.

Although not included in the original recipe, a sugar cube, with or without one or two dashes of Angostura bitters, can be placed in the glass before pouring. Some people also choose to add the absinthe to the champagne, as many brands of absinthe will float on the surface of the drink for a short time if poured gently, creating a pleasing visual effect.

Hemingway's sage advice on overindulgence was always to do sober what you said you'd do drunk. That would teach you to keep your mouth shut.

ZOMBIE

1 measure of white rum
1 measure of golden rum
1 measure of dark rum
½ measure of cherry brandy
½ measure of apricot brandy
2 measures of pineapple juice
1 measure of orange juice
½ measure of papaya juice
⅓ measure of overproof rum (the highest proof you can find)
Juice of one lime
1 sprig of mint
1 slice of lime
1 slice of pineapple

Place all ingredients except the overproof rum in a shaker with a glass of crushed ice. Shake well. Pour into a Collins glass then float the overproof rum on the surface using a long-handled bar spoon. Garnish with a sprig of mint and slices of lime and pineapple. Add straws. Tim-ber!

Hollywood's Don the Beachcomber Restaurant was one of the first establishments in the USA to offer customers a taste of the South Sea Islands, with rum cocktails a speciality. Don claimed to have originated sixty-three new cocktails, including the Zombie, put together in 1934 for a patron who complained that his hangover was making him feel like a zombie. The drink then achieved national celebrity when it was served at the Hurricane Bar at the New York World's Fair in 1939. Don's rival, Vic Bergeron, was unimpressed and commented that he thought it was just too strong.

CORPSE REVIVER

1 measure of gin
1 measure of Cointreau
1 measure of Lillet Blanc
1 drop of absinthe or Pernod
2 measures of fresh lemon juice
1 maraschino cherry

Fill a mixing glass two-thirds full with ice and add all the ingredients. Stir well for at least thirty seconds. Strain into a chilled Cocktail glass and garnish with a cherry.

The Corpse Reviver is one of the oldest cocktails from the family of drinks classed as 'eye-openers', 'pick-me-ups' or 'hair of the dog'. Corpse Revivers were popular in Europe from at least the late 1800s and boasted a variety of ingredients, although many were brandy-based. The recipe here is based on a version first perfected by Harry Craddock in the 1930s. Craddock was a US citizen who fled his homeland following the onset of Prohibition. In 1920 he joined the American Bar at the Savoy Hotel, London, and went on to become one of the most noted cocktail-makers of the 1920s and 1930s.

According to Craddock, the Corpse Reviver was 'to be taken before 11 a.m., or whenever steam or energy are needed'. He also added a warning that 'four of these in quick succession will unrevive the corpse again'.

STINGER

2 measures of brandy
1 measure of white crème
de menthe

Pour the brandy and crème de menthe into a cocktail shaker filled with cracked ice and shake vigorously. Strain into a frosted Martini glass. Alternatively, fill a Highball glass with ice, pour over the brandy and crème de menthe and stir well before serving.

Invented around 1900, the Stinger can be employed as a curative but is also excellent as a post-dinner drink, since it aids digestion, and can be thoroughly enjoyed at any time. It was at the peak of its popularity during Prohibition. Like the Martini it had a number of literary devotees, including Ian Fleming, Somerset Maugham and Evelyn Waugh. An acquaintance of Waugh's, on hearing of his predilection for the drink, claimed it was just the sort of affectation they had come to expect from the writer.

In *High Society* Bing Crosby's character, Dexter Haven, explains the name of the cocktail to a sore-headed and remorseful Grace Kelly. 'It's a Stinger. It removes the sting.' The taking of alcohol to lessen the effects of a hangover is based on the principle of like curing like and the antique saying that you can cure a dog's bite with its fur – a piece of folk wisdom that, it has been claimed, goes back to Aristophanes in the fifth century BC.

The Stinger was also Billie Holiday's favourite cocktail. Sinatra once said of her, 'It was Billie Holiday, who I first heard in 52nd Street clubs in the early thirties, who was and still remains the greatest single musical influence on me.' It was around that time that he got involved in one of his first public fights after strenuously berating two men who were talking too loudly during one of her sets at the Onyx Club.

RED DEVIL

2¼ measures of Irish whiskey
1¾ measures of clam juice
1¾ measures of tomato juice
A few dashes of Worcestershire sauce
1 pinch of ground pepper
Juice of quarter of a lime

Shake all the ingredients with plenty of ice – only briefly and not harshly – and strain into a large Cocktail glass.

A potent hangover restorative that also serves as an excellent appetizer or aperitif, the Red Devil was developed as a speciality of Le Périgord Restaurant at the Sherry-Netherland Hotel, New York City.

PRAIRIE OYSTER

2 measures of cognac
1 egg yolk
3 dashes of malt vinegar
2 dashes of Tabasco sauce
2 dashes of Worcestershire sauce
Salt and pepper

Carefully place the egg yolk at the bottom of a Cocktail glass. Add the other ingredients slowly, ensuring the yolk remains whole. Season and drink in one.

Consuming a Prairie Oyster is an act of bravery, although many people swear to its effectiveness as a restorative. It is sometimes taken *sans* cognac as a non-alcoholic remedy, eggs having long been thought to aid recovery the morning after the night before. In that case, it is not a hair of the dog.

Listing the ingredients alone is enough to provoke a shudder. The drink has even less charm when the name is explained: it is Old West slang for a bull's testicle.

JILLY'S

'This is my hang-out too.' – Frank Sinatra

This was the legend printed, along with a facsimile signature, on napkins at Jilly's, and whenever Sinatra was in New York he loved to spend nights in this dim, smoke-filled 120-seat saloon at 256 West 52nd Street in Manhattan. It could be described as a piano bar – Judy Garland often sang there while drinking – a lounge, even a restaurant, but at its heart it was a saloon and a virtual shrine to Sinatra. There were pictures of him on the wall, a life-size cut-out of him in *Pal Joey* situated near the bar and a framed photograph on the piano. Roped off from the main rooms was Sinatra's inner sanctum – a back room, the portal to which was guarded by a burly *maître d'*. Beyond the red velvet rope was Sinatra's booth, a long table against the back wall. He had his own personal chair– a blue high-backed, imitation-leather armchair – that was brought out when he arrived and put away when he left. The owner, Jilly Rizzo, had a matching throne that he would pull up beside Sinatra's. There was an electric sign outside that read 'Home of the King'.

Gay Talese described a night at Jilly's in a famous *Esquire* article from 1966, 'Frank Sinatra Has a Cold'. Talese saw dozens of men and women crowded outside the bar hoping to gain entry and perhaps catch a glimpse of Sinatra holding court. Making it past the doormen was an achievement. Seeing him and his companions at his table while being crushed at the bar was enough to send most home happy. Being the recipient of a nod, a wave or even a smile made ordinary folk feel as though they had been sanctified. 'Frank,' Jilly Rizzo would say, 'you purify the goddamn room.'

The owner of Jilly's was Ermenigildo Rizzo. The son of immigrant parents, he was born in 1917 and raised in New York's Lower West Side. In his youth he worked with his father delivering Italian ice to cafés in the area. A large man, sometimes mistaken for a rhino, he had vague plans to become a pro boxer before a stint in the army, followed by a succession of bartending jobs and the opening of his own saloon. Sinatra first spotted him sitting ringside at a show at the Copacabana in the 1950s and asked to be introduced. By that time Jilly already had a glass eye and two arrests for assault. He became one of Sinatra's closest friends and an unofficial bodyguard.

Jilly's had everything Sinatra liked in a hang-out: an interesting late-night crowd (politicians, working girls, musicians and alleged associates of the New York crime families); top piano player (Bobby Cole); a discreet and accommodating management with a relaxed attitude to official licensing hours; and good food if he required it. Sinatra rated Jilly's chicken chow mein as some of the best in the city.

Jilly and his bar received several name-checks in song, and not just from Frank – Sammy Davis mentions the saloon twice in his version of 'Me and My Shadow' – and Sinatra began one live recording at the Sands by announcing to his Vegas audience 'Welcome to Jilly's West.' Jilly had bit-parts in several films and appeared behind his own bar in the 1962 version of *The Manchurian Candidate* telling a story that initiates one of Lawrence Harvey's hypnotic trances.

Another reason that Sinatra loved Jilly's company (apart from his obvious usefulness in dealing with perceived trouble-makers) was his Runyonesque mangling of the English language. 'When he comes in my room,' he said of Sinatra, 'it's like a terrific thrill for me which I am a guy that has seen a lot.' His non-sequiturs were legendary. Sitting in another bar in the 1970s, P.J. Clarke's, Sinatra was debating the relative merits of F. Scott Fitzgerald and Ernest Hemingway with sportswriter Jimmy Cannon. Cannon favoured Hemingway. When Jilly Rizzo returned to the table, Sinatra asked for his vote. 'What about you, Jilly? Hemingway or Fitzgerald?'

'Hey, no contest,' said Jilly. 'Ella all the way.'

During its heyday in the 1960s Jilly's was the place to be,

especially if Sinatra was in town. Irish Mike, the *maître d'*, told *Esquire* that on evenings when Sinatra was at his table 'the place is New Year's Eve'.

During the 1970s Jilly's closed, and its owner moved to Palm Springs in order to be close at hand for Sinatra. Rizzo died on his seventy-fifth birthday, in 1992, when his car was hit by a drunk driver. He is buried in the Sinatra family plot. Dean Martin reopened the saloon, made over as a restaurant, Dino's, but in 1985 it became the Russian Samovar Restaurant, co-owned by Mikhail Baryshnikov. Some of the original bar and fittings were retained, and disciples would book a table just to be able to touch the wood and remember – or imagine – the old times.

BOILERMAKER

1 glass of beer
1 shot of whiskey or Scotch

Technically a beer cocktail, the boilermaker is a combination of beer and whiskey, often drunk by men stopping off at local saloons on the way back from (or sometimes on the way to) a hard-working shift. The whiskey is usually downed in one and then chased with cold beer, as demonstrated by Marlon Brando in *On the Waterfront* (1954). Some practitioners insist that the beer, like the whiskey, should be finished in one go; others allow that more time can be taken finishing the chaser. Some choose to sip the beer first and then pour the whiskey in and drink the mixture; others drop the shot glass into the beer glass, a 'depth charge'.

When Sinatra talked fondly of saloons or called himself the Saloon Singer, he had in mind the kind of place, usually in the heart of a city, where men might gather in personal solitude, light a cigarette and order a boilermaker. Jilly's was something like one of those places, but maybe only on nights when Sinatra had not brought the crowds in.

JIMMY VAN HEUSEN

'I'm a whore for my music.'

Born Edward Chester Babcock in Syracuse, New York, in 1913, Van Heusen went on to become one the most popular American composers of the 1940s and 1950s and beyond. He renamed himself aged sixteen, taking his surname from a shirt company, and began writing and performing songs in college. Sinatra first met him the late 1930s when he just starting out and desperate for any singing work. Van Heusen was working as a song-plugger for Remick Music during the day and moonlighting as an elevator operator in a hotel at night. It was inevitable that they would become friends – both men had a voracious appetite for women and hard liquor and a mutual admiration for each other's talents.

Van Heusen was mightily successful in his own right. His chief collaborator between 1940 and 1953 was the lyricist Johnny Burke, and they produced several smash hits. From 1954 he wrote with Sammy Cahn – their songs for Sinatra during the Capitol years helped in Sinatra's great revival of fortunes.

As well as being one of the few men who could match Sinatra in his drinking and womanizing, he was a consummate architect of melodies, and he recorded more Jimmy Van Heusen songs than any other single composer, something in the order of eighty-five in total. These included 'Come Fly with Me', 'Only the Lonely', 'Come Dance with Me', 'No One Cares', 'All the Way' and 'Ring-a-Ding-Ding!'

Van Heusen was a friend and ally as well as a collaborator. He was a founder member of the Holmby Hills Rat Pack, and it was Van Heusen who took Sinatra in when times got really hard. Sinatra stayed with Van Heusen at Jimmy's 57th Street apartment in New York, drinking most nights until the early hours. Van Heusen didn't mind the drinking sessions; he even encouraged friends to join the parties and help keep Frank distracted. It didn't always work, however. It was Jimmy who rushed him to hospital after a failed suicide attempt during the Ava Gardner affair.

He began shaving his head in his twenties when premature baldness struck – an unusual move at the time – and was nobody's idea of handsome. He was also a hypochondriac who kept a medical dictionary by his bed, regularly injected himself with vitamins and painkillers and had a number of medical procedures for afflictions both real and imagined. He was, however, rich, successful and flew his own airplane (during the Second World War he had worked as a test pilot for Lockheed), and consequently he was rarely without a female companion.

As well as for Sinatra he had also penned a number of hits for Bing Crosby, and the two had become close friends. In 1956 Crosby and Van Heusen flew out to see their friend during a stint at the Sands. Crosby and Van Heusen had an ulterior motive – word was that Sinatra was on the verge of collapse after too many late nights, virtually no sleep and a great deal of sauce. On arrival it was obvious to them that he looked and sounded exhausted, and when they went backstage Crosby immediately offered to take over the gig so that Sinatra could rest his voice. Sinatra declined but told Crosby that he wanted to talk to him confidentially and asked to meet him in a restaurant after the show. Crosby agreed, thinking it might be a good opportunity to try to talk some sense into him. A few hours later they met up, but before Crosby could say anything Sinatra looked at him and said, 'Bing, we've got to do something about Van Heusen. He's not taking very good care of himself.'

Van Heusen's quote about being a whore for his music had everything to do with the fact that he sometimes had to put up with some very bad behaviour on Sinatra's part. Kitty Kelley, in *His Way,* recounted the occasion in the early 1960s when Sinatra had an altercation with, of all people, Desi Arnaz. Sinatra came off worse in a tense exchange of words in the Indian Wells

Country Club in California. Van Heusen was present and urged Sinatra to forget the whole thing, but he wouldn't. After returning to Van Heusen's Palm Desert house for late drinks with two female companions Sinatra disappeared into Van Heusen's den. On the wall was an original Norman Rockwell painting of Jimmy in a pyjama top, sitting at his piano. A personal gift from the artist, it was one of his most treasured possessions. Sinatra tore it to strips with a knife. When one of the women asked Van Heusen why he put up with being treated like that he sighed and explained, 'Because he sings my songs. That's why.'

Little wonder then that, despite the many good times they shared, Van Heusen's advice on what to do when Sinatra was drunk was short and sweet. 'Disappear!'

Sinatra and Bing Crosby digging each other's crooning in *High Society*, 1956

High Society

Saloons were where he started out. They were in his blood, and he never lost his love of a good old-fashioned bar, but, of course, he also frequented more fancy watering holes, usually in the company of other celebrities. As a rising star he was required to be seen at celebrity hang-outs such as the Stork Club or El Morocco, and for the kid from Hoboken these apparently sophisticated and undeniably glamorous New York establishments had an irresistible appeal. As well as a patron he also attended clubs like the Copacabana as a performer.

When he made his move to Hollywood he was encouraged to be seen at such places as Ciro's, clinking glasses with fellow stars of screen and stage, but for Sinatra there was an inherent danger lurking. Exclusive and upmarket clubs attracted a certain class of newspaper people – gossip columnists. The nightclub management encouraged their presence (name-dropping in newspapers was invaluable PR for them), but Sinatra detested them. Many stars were willing to play the game and flatter the likes of Hedda Hopper, mindful of their power. In return the columnists would overlook certain indiscretions. Frank was unwilling or unable to accommodate them. He had strong feelings about such people, and after several drinks he would express these feelings in too public a place. He also lacked discretion in other matters, often initiating and carrying on brief extramarital flings in nightclubs. The inevitable happened when a particularly vicious hack who had taken to needling him in the press was confronted and 'became punched' in a nightclub parking lot. Some in the press never forgave him.

The older, more mature, post-comeback Sinatra was more at ease with himself and the world in general. If the mood took him he was able to spend an evening at Chasen's or some other Beverley Hills celebrity watering hole surrounded by a reliable, hand-picked entourage, secure in the knowledge that little in the way of havoc was likely to occur or be reported.

21 CLUB

Originally one of America's most infamous speakeasies, the 21 Club opened on 1 January 1930, equipped with its own disappearing bar and secret wine cellar. Charlie Berns and Jack Kreindler had opened a bar called the Puncheon on West 49th Street in 1926. Unfortunately it turned out to be on land that had been earmarked as the site of the Rockefeller Centre. They received $11,000 compensation and used it to move three blocks north to 21 West 52nd Street. They employed architect Frank Buchanan to incorporate a complex system of camouflaged doors, invisible chutes, revolving bars and a hidden wine cellar in which they could secrete illegal booze. Raids were frequent, but staff could claim, semi-truthfully, that there was no liquor on the premises – the actual wine cellar had been constructed in the basement of number 19 next door. The premises were conjoined by a specially constructed two-ton concrete door. The cellar held 2,000 cases of wine and was eventually used to house some of the private wine collections of many of the rich, famous and powerful, from Mae West, Elizabeth Taylor and Sophia Loren to Aristotle Onassis and Richard Nixon.

The new club quickly became an exclusive venue for many of the rich young socialites of the Roaring Twenties. A short walk from the Broadway theatre district, it was also frequented by celebrities from show business, as well as sports stars, literary types and big names from business and politics.

Al Jolson, Mae West and the Marx Brothers were all early members, and later the likes of Frank, Sammy and Gene Kelly. Robert Benchley, Dorothy Parker and Ernest Hemingway all drank there, as did the Kennedys and Richard Nixon. Bogart, too, was a regular. His table, number 30, was known as 'Bogie's Corner', and it was where he sat on his first ever date with a young model-turned-actress by the name of Bacall. Sinatra's table was number 14.

SOUTH SIDE

1½ measures of gin 1½ measures of lemon juice Fresh mint Sugar	*Place the gin, lemon juice, a small handful of fresh mint leaves and sugar to taste in a chilled shaker and mix briskly. Add three or four ice cubes to a stemless Cocktail glass and pour over.*

This simple and elegant cocktail was a speciality of the 21 Club and was even more popular when not constructed with bathtub gin.

CHASEN'S

Located in West Hollywood, at 9039 Beverley Boulevard near Beverley Hills, Chasen's Restaurant grew from humble beginnings into one of the glamour spots for the Hollywood elite. As well as being the home of the Flame of Love cocktail it was the place where Ronald Reagan proposed to Nancy (the booth was later presented to the Reagan Presidential Library), where Jimmy Stewart held his bachelor party and where countless other star-studded celebrations were hosted.

Originally opened as a barbecue stand by comedian Dave Chasen in 1936, it served hearty food with specialities that included seafood on ice and Hobo Steak – New York beef cooked in butter, served on toast points with soufflé potatoes and creamed spinach. The highlight for many was Dave Chasen's Chilli, a favourite of both JFK and Elizabeth Taylor, who had portions frozen and flown out to Rome while filming *Cleopatra*.

The list of famous names who sat in its exclusive front room is probably unmatched – regulars included Humphrey Bogart, Jack Benny, George Burns and Gracie Allen, Gregory Peck, Bob Hope, Groucho Marx, Alfred Hitchcock, Walt Disney, Marilyn Monroe, Shirley Temple, Cary Grant, W.C. Fields, James Cagney, Clark Gable, Kirk Douglas and F. Scott Fitzgerald. In later decades the likes of John Travolta, Mel Gibson, Jack Nicholson and Warren Beatty spent many evenings there. Many of the celebrities had individual booths named after them, and for many years Chasen's was the venue for a celebrated Academy Awards party.

The original Chasen's closed in 1995, although the name was licensed to another location. In an auction of memorabilia in 1999 a photograph of Sinatra and pals at play in the restaurant sold for a bargain $225.

CHASEN'S BANANA PUNCH

1 measure of vodka 1 dash of abricotine Juice of half a lime 1 sprig of mint	*Fill a Collins glass with crushed ice. Pour over the alcohol, squeeze the lime, then top up with soda water and present with a sprig of mint.*

Naturally Chasen's used only the finest ingredients in their signature cocktails, and abricotine is a French brandy liqueur that is considered to be among the finest examples of flavoured liqueurs. Somewhat confusingly, however, despite the fact that this fine cocktail was described as a 'banana punch', abricotine is distinctly apricot flavoured. It was also prepared individually rather than in batches like many punches. It remains delicious despite any confusion.

PUMP ROOM

Sinatra knew bars, saloons and more salubrious drinking establishments all over the USA and made a point of finding them wherever he travelled. In Chicago he was known to patronize the famous Pump Room. Ernie Byfield, the man behind the Pump Room, had a curious inspiration for his establishment – he claimed to have modelled it on the eighteenth-century Pump Room in Bath, England, a place where Queen Anne and other London socialites would gather to gossip while taking the waters.

Established in 1938 as a restaurant inside the Ambassador East Hotel in Chicago's Gold Coast area, it rapidly became the preferred stopping-off point for celebrities changing trains in Chicago while travelling between New York and Los Angeles. Stars of the stage and screen in the 1930s, 1940s and 1950s would be ushered by Ernie into the legendary Booth One. This was the place where Humphrey Bogart and Lauren Bacall celebrated their wedding, as did Robert Wagner and Natalie Wood, and Sinatra was often ensconced there. The original booth was donated to the Chicago History Museum. Famous guests included Marlene Dietrich, Cole Porter, Bette Davis, Judy Garland, Paul Newman and Joanne Woodward, Lena Horne, Elizabeth Taylor, Dean Martin and Jerry Lewis, Joan Crawford, Tallulah Bankhead, Josephine Baker, Peggy Lee, Audrey Hepburn, Alfred Hitchcock, John Steinbeck and Robert Redford. Many signed the famous signature book, which was, unfortunately, urinated on by another guest, John Barrymore, after a surfeit of champagne.

Ernie Byfield himself had a fine sense of the theatrical, a fact reflected in some of the house cocktails and the Pump Room's famous flambé dishes, which helped start a culinary trend across post-war America.

The Pump Room was celebrated by being name-checked in at least two songs associated with Sinatra, 'Chicago (That Toddlin' Town)' and 'My Kind of Town (Chicago Is)'. The entrance is also immortalized in a scene from Hitchcock's *North by Northwest,* and Phil Collins named the album *No Jacket Required* after an occasion when he was denied entry.

BATH CURE

1½ measures of Jamaican rum 1 measure of Puerto Rican gold rum 2 measures of light (white) rum 1 measure of overproof rum 1½ measures of brandy 1½ measures of vodka ½ measure of grenadine 1 measure of fresh lemon juice 1 measure of fresh pineapple juice 1 measure of fresh orange juice ½ measure of fresh lime juice 1 slice of lime 1 maraschino cherry	*Fill a blender quarter full of cracked ice. Add all the liquid ingredients and blend well before pouring into a large Cocktail glass. Decorate with fruit and present with two straws.*

A Pump Room speciality that had a suitably dramatic presentation – the glass was brought to the table encased in a hollow container filled with shaved ice, which was decorated with streaks of red and green food colouring.

SHERRY FLIP

1½ measures of sherry 3 dashes of crème de cacao 1 egg 1 heaped teaspoon of granulated sugar Nutmeg	*Place all the ingredients in an electric blender along with half a cup of shaved ice. Mix well and pour into a chilled champagne goblet. Top with two or three pinches of nutmeg before presenting.*

In the Pump Room cocktail-making and presentation always involved baroque elements, and this is one of the few cocktail recipes that specifies the use of an electric blender in its construction.

EL MATADOR

El Matador, a nightclub that combined elements of the saloon and the salon, was the creation of Barnaby Conrad, a man described by *The Paris Review* as 'one of the bon vivant-ist of all modern bon vivant writers'. As well as a novelist and club owner he was a diplomat (serving as US Vice-Consul in Spain), a bullfighter and an accomplished artist (portraits by him of some of his famous friends hang on the walls of the National Portrait Gallery in Washington). The son of a wealthy banker, he was born in San Francisco in 1922 and grew up in Hillsborough, California. Educated at the Taft School, Connecticut, he spent a year at the University of North Carolina before winning a place at Yale to study art.

He spent the summer before going up to Yale in Mexico where, inspired by Hemingway's *Death in the Afternoon* and emboldened by drink, he leaped into a bullring and challenged a bull using his raincoat as a cape. Rather than being outraged, the bullfighter whose turn he had rudely interrupted was so impressed by the young man's bravado that he offered to give him lessons. Unfortunately Conrad was gored through the knee during the first coaching session, an injury that earned him exemption from wartime military service.

After graduating from Yale in 1943 he worked for the State Department in Spain and resumed his bullfighting training under the matador Juan Belmonte, who had featured in Hemingway's book. He fought under the name 'El Niño de California'. In 1945 he was awarded the ears of a bull he had killed. After the war he lived for a time in Peru, playing piano in a hotel bar, painting portraits and writing for various magazines. For a short time he was also personal secretary to the novelist Sinclair Lewis. He became a literary celebrity in his own right following the publication of the novel *Matador* in 1952. The book was based on the death in the bullring of Manuel Laureano Rodríguez Sánchez, a legendary matador known as 'Manolete'. It sold three million copies and spent fifty weeks on national bestseller lists in the USA.

The idea for a nightclub came after a visit from his Boston-based publisher Paul Brooks. Following dinner Conrad asked Brooks what he would like to do for the rest of the evening. Brooks requested they find 'an attractive bar and listen to a good piano'. When Conrad claimed he could not immediately think of anywhere suitable, Brooks suggested, not quite seriously, 'Why don't you start one?' Conrad eventually found and bought (using the proceeds from his book sales) an old Mexican dance hall in the Barbary Coast area of San Francisco and set about creating 'an elegant bar with a torero motif'. Claiming that he found most nightclubs garish and uninviting, he aimed to create a chic and comfortable environment, a fine piano bar with a baby grand, a place 'where attractive and interesting people could congregate over a Martini'.

El Matador opened its doors in 1958. It was decorated throughout with bullfighting paintings, many by Conrad himself, but also including an original Picasso. There was a thirty-by-thirteen-foot mural of the bull ring in Seville and a life-size portrait of Manolete. There was also a large glass aviary containing a number of colourful and noisy parrots, including Conrad's beloved Macgregor, a macaw he had unwittingly bought from smugglers and who had been taken into custody by the FBI (Conrad appeared as a federal witness in court proceedings against the smuggling ring in order to have the bird returned). The men's room was covered with blackboard slate, and chalk trays were provided so that patrons could indulge their literary and artistic bents. Directly above the bar was a magnificent stuffed bull's head, originally a prop from the Tyrone Power film *Blood and Sand*. A large piece of rubber tubing had been secreted in one nostril, fed back through the hollow head, across the length of the bar and into the kitchen beyond. When the opportunity presented itself the *maître d'*, John Clarke, would light a cigarette in the kitchen and blow smoke down the tube. The effect caused consternation among some drinkers, especially those who had overindulged and especially when Bill Eddison the bartender would insist, after considering the head, that he could see nothing unusual. Many of the staff were characters in their own right, including accountant Grace West, a middle-aged bohemian who wrote poetry, janitor Jack Negherbon, who bred parrots and played guitar, and the dark-eyed waitress Olga, who claimed to be the niece of an ex-president of Peru. Olga's English was limited, and she would present a plate of calamari as 'worms'. The piano in one corner of the room, crucial to the ambience, was played by the man described by the *San Francisco Chronicle* as 'the eminent saloon pianist' John Horton Cooper. Cooper had the reputation of being absolutely imperturbable; whatever drunken antics took place around him he remained unmoved and had a standard comment for most occasions, 'One never knows, do one?' It became a popular catchphrase around the Barbary Coast.

The club rapidly became the place to be seen, one early report noting that Sinatra, Hermione Gingold, Zsa Zsa Gabor and William Randolph Hearst Jr all arrived within minutes of each other in a single night. Show-business types flocked there – Orson Welles, Bing Crosby, David Niven, Lucille Ball, Marilyn Monroe, John Wayne, Robert Mitchum, Marlene Dietrich, Tallulah Bankhead and Judy Garland. The literary elite were also in attendance, Conrad being on good drinking terms with John Steinbeck, Jack Kerouac, Sinclair Lewis, Truman Capote and Noël Coward (whom Conrad described as being 'like a good Martini' in honour of his extra-dry wit). André Previn, Errol Garner, George Shearing and Duke Ellington were among those whom John Horton Cooper would allow to take over the piano temporarily. Wallis Simpson visited, and gangster Mickey Cohen chose the Mat, as it was called by fans, as the venue to celebrate his release from Alcatraz. Of course, Ava Gardner adored everything about El Matador. Sinatra may have been less keen, but he was, nevertheless, in regular attendance throughout the club's glory days in the late 1950s through to the early 1970s.

By 1972 Conrad had moved to Santa Barbara, where he founded the Santa Barbara Writers' Conference, which continues to this day. Conrad passed away on 12 February 2013.

BLOOD AND SAND

1 measure of Scotch
1 measure of cherry brandy
1 measure of sweet vermouth
1 measure of fresh orange juice
1 orange slice

Add the liquid ingredients to a cocktail shaker half filled with cracked ice. Shake well, strain into a chilled Cocktail glass and garnish with the orange slice.

Described by the *Wall Street Journal* as 'strange but delicious', this classic Scotch cocktail was created in honour of Rudolph Valentino's silent classic of the same name, a torrid tale of a bullfighter embroiled in a tragic love triangle. The film was based on a book by the Spanish journalist, politician and novelist Vicente Blasco Ibáñez. Ibáñez achieved bestseller status in the USA in the early years of the twentieth century and had several of his novels adapted by Hollywood. As well as *Blood and Sand*, which was remade in Technicolor in 1941, the other great movie success from one of his novels was *The Four Horsemen of the Apocalypse*, also starring Valentino.

A popular joke from the cocktail's heyday involves a Hollywood type (usually a screenwriter) who becomes enamoured of the drink and pesters the barman for the recipe. The barman is reluctant to reveal trade secrets but is eventually persuaded to talk after the Hollywood type brandishes a $100 bill. 'So what's in the drink?' demands the customer. 'Well,' says the barman, pocketing the money, 'there's blood in it . . . and sand.' Luckily it actually contains neither.

MATADOR

2 measures of white
(blanco) tequila
3 measures of pineapple
juice
Juice of half a lime
1 slice of pineapple
(optional)

Combine the ingredients in a shaker with crushed ice. Shake well and serve in a chilled Cocktail glass. A single pineapple slice may be added as garnish.

Ava Gardner fell in love with Spain and Spanish culture and visited often throughout the 1950s. She learned flamenco dancing and even tried her hand at bullfighting. She also had a number of front-page affairs with bullfighters, the most famous being a fling with Luis Miguel Dominguín. In September 1955 *Time* magazine described how a young matador, César Girón, presented the bloody ears and tail of a bull he had dispatched to Ava who clutched an ear to her lips for a long kiss as the crowd cheered. Her admission of an affair during the making of 1954's *The Barefoot Contessa* was one of the reasons for the breakdown of her marriage to Sinatra. She said he never forgave her. It was only one of many reasons, however.

According to the *Maryland News* in 1955, 'The West Coast film colony is serving as a guinea pig for the introduction of a new drink called the Matador.' Obviously a close relation of the Margarita, this very simple cocktail may well have been inspired by Conrad's book. The *Maryland News* went on to report that the recipe 'calls for a jigger of tequila, two jiggers of pineapple, a squeeze of lime and crushed ice. Stir like crazy, then serve.'

CHI CHI

The Chi Chi was a Palm Canyon Drive supper club that during the 1940s and 1950s was a popular venue for movie folks, musicians and the occasional gangster element. It opened in 1938 and soon became a premier venue for touring jazz and pop performers. The owner, Irwin Schulman, was a friend of Howard Hughes, who was a regular. He rented no less than three properties in Palm Springs, and when he was due to visit he would call Schulman to arrange for May (a trusted Chi Chi employee) to disinfect whichever house he would be staying in. Hughes brought a succession of starlets to the club and entertained them in a private back booth. The club orchestra usually finished at 1.30 a.m. but were required to play on past that time if Hughes requested it, being allowed to leave only when Hughes had completed his seduction.

The gangster element included Mickey Cohen and Sam Giancana. Their regular appearances meant that Schulman was also obliged to entertain the two plain-clothed policeman who visited at least three times a night to take notes.

The club's Starlight Room, which contained a huge circular stage with a dome full of sparkling lights, attracted top musical acts from Sophie Tucker to Louis Armstrong, Nat King Cole to Dorothy Dandridge. It was here that movie stars, directors and producers such as Cecil B. DeMille and studio heads, including Jack Warner, would gather. Local real-estate agents would take prospective clients along to help seal deals. The Chi Chi was often used as a place to rehearse and preview Vegas reviews and was one of the first Palm Springs clubs to stay open all year round. Out of season the full orchestra might, however, be reduced to a trio who played in the lounge.

In 1946 Sinatra was seen in the club in the company of fellow MGM star Lana Turner. She already had a house in Palm Springs, and Sinatra would buy his first property there the following year. Their on–off dalliance was an open secret in the film community and was hinted at in the press. It was the first public hint that his carefully cultivated image as a happily married man was a sham, although his marriage to Nancy would somehow survive another four years. Another conquest from that time, actress Shirley Ballard, recalled succumbing to his charms after Sinatra took her to the Chi Chi and ended the evening serenading her with 'I've Got a Crush on You'.

The Chi Chi closed in 1965, but Schulman had already moved on to bigger and better things. In 1959 he had started work on what would become the Riviera Palm Springs Hotel, where Sinatra would eventually become a star attraction.

CHI CHI COCKTAIL

1½ measures of vodka
4 measures of pineapple juice
1 measure of cream of coconut
1 slice of pineapple
1 maraschino cherry

Blend the liquid ingredients in an electric blender with a small cup of ice. Pour the resulting slush into a large wine glass and garnish with the pineapple slice and cherry before presenting.

A blended cocktail that is a close relative of the later Piña Colada – but with vodka rather than rum as the base spirit – the Chi Chi enjoyed a brief vogue in the 1950s (and was sometimes regarded as an exotic 'tiki drink' like the Mai Tai and the Zombie) before falling into obscurity.

CIRO'S

Ciro's nightclub first opened its doors in January 1940 at 8433 Sunset Boulevard on Hollywood's famous Sunset Strip. It was Lana Turner's favourite nightspot and became a popular Hollywood hang-out for celebrities throughout the 1940s and 1950s. Sinatra was often in attendance, rubbing shoulders with the likes of Joan Crawford, Betty Grable, Marlene Dietrich, Cary Grant, George Raft, Peter Lawford,

Sinatra muses on the
September of his years, 1970

Jimmy Stewart and Spencer Tracy. A young John F. Kennedy dined there in the late 1940s during his first trip to Hollywood.

It was initially brought into being by Billy Wilkerson, publisher of *The Hollywood Reporter*. The venue had previously been a high-stakes gambling club much favoured by movie moguls such as David O. Selznick and Harry Cohen. Closed down by the vice squad in 1938, it reopened a year later as Club Saville. Its main attraction was a glass dance floor, which was fitted over a pool filled with live carp, but the Saville failed, and when Wilkerson took over the lease he gave the interior a lavish, baroque makeover. He also eventually hired an experienced manager, Herman Hoover. Hoover had begun his nightclub career running the Silver Slipper, a Prohibition-era New York club owned by Arnold Rothstein and Lucky Luciano; for a time he had also run Harlem's Cotton Club before moving to Los Angeles in the late 1930s.

As an extremely active member of the Hollywood social scene, Wilkerson knew the value of being seen in the right places and helped ensure that being spotted at Ciro's guaranteed column inches from regular patrons such as Hedda Hopper, Louella Parsons and Florabel Muir. He also made sure that the live entertainment at the club was the finest available. Xavier Cugat performed regularly, as did Nat King Cole, Dinah Washington, Mae West, Desi Arnaz, Cab Calloway, Peggy Lee and Edith Piaf. Judy Garland first appeared there as a teenager on a Wednesday Amateur Night (she won). Herman Hoover hosted Dean Martin's second wedding at the club in 1949, the following year Lewis and Martin débuted their act at Ciro's. Within months they were the highest-paid double act in show business, able to command fees of $100,000 per engagement, but when they returned to Ciro's they wanted only their original fee of $7,000 for one week. Sammy Davis also got one of his first big breaks there and marked his return to the world with a barnstorming performance at the club after his near-fatal car accident. It was also where the nightclub scenes in *Meet Danny Wilson* were filmed.

Sinatra was famously photographed at his table with Nancy and his statuette on the night he was awarded a special Oscar for *The House I Live In* in 1946, but being a regular patron at an establishment that welcomed

127

and encouraged gossip columnists was always going to mean potential trouble for him. On 8 April 1947, in the car park at Ciro's, Sinatra punched out Lee Mortimer, a Hearst columnist who had been needling Sinatra for months in print about his liberal politics and failing career. Mortimer took Sinatra to court, and it was the beginning of his fractious relationship with some sections of the press.

By the mid-1950s almost all of Sunset Strip's upmarket nightclubs had disappeared. Ciro's lasted longer than most but eventually closed its doors for good in 1957. In the early 1970s the Comedy Store opened on the site.

Although they have a name in common (almost certainly not an accident), Billy Wilkerson's Ciro's had no actual connection with Ciro's of London – a fashionable nightclub established in 1915 that styled itself 'the famous London rendezvous of smart society'. The head bartender at Ciro's of London was Harry MacElhone, the author of *Harry of Ciro's ABC of Mixing Cocktails*, who went on to even more wonderful things after moving to Paris to open what would become Harry's Bar.

AFTER DINNER SPECIAL

⅓ measure of Benedictine
⅓ measure of Cointreau
⅓ measure of yellow chartreuse

Pour each of the ingredients carefully (in the above order) into a chilled Cocktail glass to create a pleasing effect of layering.

Ciro's post-dinner special was a thing of beauty and a tribute to the skill and artistry of the barman, on whom it depended for its visual effect.

VESUVIUS

1 measure of grappa	*Pour all the ingredients into a shaker filled*
1 measure of Benedictine	*with ice. Stir well and present, strained, in a*
¼ measure of triple sec	*Cocktail glass.*
Juice of half a lemon	

The Pompeii Room was part of Ciro's and had its own individual signature cocktail named in honour of the world's most famous volcano, which erupted briefly in 1944. 'Versuvinum' was a name found engraved on wine jars uncovered at Pompeii, site of the most famous eruption in AD 79 – it could well be the first example of a trademark.

STORK CLUB

'To millions and millions of people all over the world the Stork symbolizes and epitomizes the de-luxe upholstery of quintessentially urban existence. It means fame, it means wealth, it means an elegant way of life among celebrated folk.' – Lucius Beebe

Described by journalist Walter Winchell as 'New York's New Yorkiest place', the Stork Club was probably the most famous and alluring nightspot in the Big Apple during a golden age of sophisticated nightlife. Opened originally in 1929, it was closed in 1931 and eventually reopened at 3 East 53rd Street, just east of Fifth Avenue, in 1934. The Stork was the baby of Sherman Billingsley, an ex-bootlegger from Oklahoma who partnered with two professional gamblers from his home state in order to open a New York restaurant. Billingsley remained the face of the Stork throughout its history, hogging the limelight and helping to keep in shadow a succession of dubious business partners.

Billingsley set out to create an American version of European café society. He believed the key to success would be to attract celebrities to his club, and he did everything he could to make this happen, confident that their presence guaranteed hangers-on and large numbers of the general public eager to glimpse their heroes at play – including regulars Joe DiMaggio and Marilyn Monroe, Frank Sinatra and the Duke and Duchess of Windsor, together with Sam Goldwyn, Clark Gable, Artie Shaw, Ava Gardner, Barbara Stanwyck, Judy Garland, Busby Berkeley, Humphrey Bogart and Lauren Bacall, Fay Wray, Harold Lloyd and any number of stars of screen and stage. Billingsley had a long-term affair with Ethel Merman, who helped attract the Broadway crowd. Celebrity patrons received regular gifts – diamond-studded compacts, perfume, champagne, liquor – all emblazoned with the Stork Club logo. The non-famous were also treated. Sunday night was Balloon Night, and at the stroke of midnight a net suspended above the dance floor was opened, sending down dozens of balloons, each of which contained a ticket. Prizes ranged from bracelet charms through to brand-new cars; several balloons would contain a $100 bill.

To enter the club patrons would pass a fourteen-carat solid-gold chain, lifted to allow access to a small lobby with lines of telephone booths and coat-and-hat-check facilities. After this was the main bar, seventy foot long by thirty foot wide and fitted with a huge mirror that allowed patrons to admire themselves and Billingsley to keep his eye on things. The main dining-room was separate, and here customers could eat and enjoy live music and dance. The most exclusive room was the Cub Room (sometimes referred to as the 'Snub Room' by those denied entry), and it was here in relative quiet that many of the celebrities settled. It was in the Cub Room that Orson Wells and Rita Hayworth held their post-honeymoon celebrations. The Blessed Events Room was available for hire for private parties, and there was also a men-only area, the Loner's Room.

One night in 1940 Ernest Hemingway, another regular, attempted to pay his bar bill with a $100,000 cheque (well in excess of a million dollars today) received for the screen rights to *For Whom the Bell Tolls*. Billingsley politely declined to cash the cheque when it was first presented but asked Hemingway to wait until closing time at which point the transaction was completed.

For a young Sinatra hoping to establish a film career it was an important place to be noticed, and noticed he was, one newspaper reporting that his entrance was greeted by a chorus of 'female swoons' but noted later the same evening that all the men got even when Greer Garson arrived.

JULIUS SPECIAL

2 measures of Jamaican rum
1 measure of Cointreau
1 measure of fresh lime juice

Shake all the ingredients briefly with ice and strain into a chilled Cocktail glass.

Julius Corsani was a popular barman at the Stork, and his special was a favourite with celebrities and ordinary mortals alike. Many of his creations featured in Lucius Beebe's 1946 *Stork Club Bar Book*. Lucius Morris Beebe was a poet, author, photographer, railway enthusiast, gourmand and syndicated columnist who became a notable figure on the New York society scene. He wrote restaurant reviews for *Gourmand* magazine and *Playboy* – including accounts of nights in Chasen's, the Pump Room and the 21 Club – and in the 1930s and 1940s chronicled the antics of fashionable society in nightclubs such as El Morocco and the Stork Club in his 'This New York' column for the *New York Herald Tribune*. He was also the author of a history of the bowler hat, and his own sartorial elegance was celebrated in a 1939 *Life* magazine front cover titled 'Lucius Beebe Sets a Style' and by the fact that Walter Winchell christened him 'Luscious Lucian'.

He was sometimes credited with inventing the term 'café society' – he certainly popularized it – and was a natural choice to write the official bar manual for the Stork.

STORK CLUB COOLER

2 measures of gin Juice of half an orange 1 tablespoon of sugar 1 orange segment	*Add all ingredients to a shaker. Mix well with plenty of shaved ice and strain into a Collins glass. Present with fruit and straws.*

Such a simple concoction might not even seem to warrant the appellation cocktail, but this cooler was honed to perfection by Nathaniel 'Cookie' Cook, head barman at the Stork.

STORK CLUB COCKTAIL

3 measures of gin 1 measure of triple sec Juice of a small lime Juice of half an orange 1 dash of Angostura bitters Flamed orange peel	*Add all ingredients to a shaker well filled with ice. Shake vigorously and strain into a chilled Cocktail glass. Garnish with flamed orange peel.*

This, the signature cocktail of the Stork Club, is sometimes attributed to the club's service captain Eddie Whittmer but is also claimed to be another of Nathaniel Cook's creations. The drink may have had its origins in Prohibition cocktails, given the relatively heavy reliance on juice – orange juice having often been added to drinks of the period in order to mask the taste of low-grade gin of dubious provenance.

EL MOROCCO

El Morocco was a Manhattan nightclub beloved of the rich and famous and patronized by New York café society between the 1930s and 1950s.

Prohibition was a major factor in the rise of establishments such as the 21 Club, the Stork and El Morocco. The implementation of the Volstead Act spelled financial disaster for many of New York's grandest restaurants and cafés – Maxim's, Churchill's, Delmonico's and their ilk were forced to close their doors after being denied the right to serve liquor, as the proceeds from food were insufficient to maintain the high running costs. Many entrepreneurs attempted to skirt the law by opening 'nightclubs' that catered for private members – most were simply high-end speakeasies. The El Morocco opened as a speakeasy in 1931, situated at 154 East 54th Street. By the time it moved to a four-storey townhouse at 307 East 54th shortly after the Second World War the Elmo (as it was known to the cognoscenti) was already well established as one of the most glittering spots in a glittering city.

The man responsible for El Morocco was John Perona. He had arrived in the USA as a seventeen-year-old immigrant from Italy who spoke no English. He served as an apprentice on board ships, then in restaurants, graduating from busboy to waiter, head waiter and then captain at several top-end New York hotels. During Prohibition he had been involved with popular speakeasies such as the Jungle Room and the Bath Club.

El Morocco was famous for its midnight-blue ceiling decorated with blinking oriental stars, glass palm trees and the signature blue zebra-striped banquettes. The zebra motif came from Vernon MacFarlane, an Australian who decorated many Prohibition-era night spots. Although the dance floor was tiny Perona made a point of hiring top dance bands that played Latin American and American dance tunes non-stop between 10 p.m. and 4 a.m every night. Off the main room was the Champagne Room where food was served to a gentle piano-and-violin accompaniment.

Being photographed at El Morocco usually guaranteed newspaper coverage, and famous patrons appreciated the discretion of club photographer Jerome Zerbe, who always ensured that no photographs were developed showing customers in unflattering or compromising attitudes. Sinatra in his first flush of success sometimes took Nancy to dine and dance there, while Hank Sanicola (who played piano and was handy with his fists) would sit at a nearby table to keep female fans at bay.

Humphrey Bogart was once involved at an alleged incident at El Morocco and found himself in court as a witness. The judge demanded to know if Bogart had been drunk at the time? His reply was 'Isn't everybody at three o'clock in the morning?'

There is a scene in *Pal Joey* in which Sinatra's character, having just been fired, announces his intention to leave and go to the El Morocco. 'Are you kidding?' snipes a cynical showgirl. 'The only way you'll get to Morocco is if you join the Foreign Legion.'

EL MOROCCO

1½ measures of Rémy Martin VSOP	*Place all ingredients in a cocktail*
½ measure of tawny port	*shaker with plenty of cubed ice.*
¼ measure of orange curaçao	*Shake well and strain into a*
1 measure of fresh pineapple juice	*chilled champagne glass.*
1 dash of grenadine	
Juice of quarter of a lime	

According to Charles Henry Baker, a writer on food and drink for *Esquire, Gourmet* and *Town and Country* – and who counted Ernest Hemingway and William Faulkner as drinking companions – this is a recipe for a genuine North African cocktail that was acquired for him by a friend on a cruise-ship tour who stopped off in Tangiers. It was also drunk in Manhattan.

There is another cocktail called El Morocco, likely to be a more recent tribute to the club, which calls for equal measures of dry gin, dry vermouth and Campari to be poured into an ice-filled Cocktail glass then presented with an orange-quarter garnish.

COPACABANA

From the moment it opened in 1940 the Copa did its very best to present an aura of glamour and sophistication, utilizing palm trees, velvet-covered barstools and tuxedo-clad waiting staff. Situated at 10 East 60th Street in New York City, it was resolutely international in its outlook: a Brazilian-themed nightspot with two Latin house bands, a Chinese menu and an ex-pat British proprietor, Monte Proser, a well-established nightclub owner and successful press agent, whose clients had included Walt Disney and Mary Pickford.

The club immediately attracted a celebrity clientele, including Errol Flynn, Louis B. Mayer, Bette Davis, Jimmy Durante and Groucho Marx and Carmen Miranda (both of whom appeared in a 1947 film named after the club and partly shot there). It had its own radio station, which broadcast between 10 p.m. and 4 a.m. The stars were named by the presenter as they entered and encouraged to speak to the listeners at home. As well as the opportunity for star-spotting, the Copa's other chief attraction was the famous Copa Girls. Known as 'ponies' because of their relatively diminutive stature (they had to be between 5 and 5 foot 4 inches tall), they wore mink bras and panties beneath extravagant outfits usually crowned with hats bejewelled with exotic fruit. The outfits were changed every three months, and the dancers were expected to dye their hair to match them. They performed three shows nightly.

The Copa regularly attracted star performers, including Judy Garland, Dinah Shore and Edith Piaf, and also had a reputation for helping break new talent – Sammy Davis and Dean Martin and Jerry Lewis had their big breaks there, as did Tony Bennett, Perry Como, Johnny Mathis, Bobby Darin and Paul Anka.

Sinatra was a regular, both as a patron and performer. He had a particularly volatile engagement at the club in 1950. It was shortly after Nancy had announced their separation, and a hostile press was highlighting his affair with Ava. Ava was with him for the opening nights and demanded he drop the song 'Nancy (with the Laughing Face)' from his set after she heard audience members sniggering.

Reviews were mixed. The *Herald Tribune* declared that 'the music that used to hypnotize the bobbysoxers is gone from the throat'. His voice faltered, and he was forced to withdraw from five dates. On 26 April he returned, but during the third show that night the unthinkable happened: he opened his mouth and nothing came out. The Copa announced the next day that he had suffered a sub-mucosal haemorrhage of the throat and had been ordered by a doctor to rest for at least two weeks. It was a terrifying time for Sinatra, but, of course, he recovered and would return in triumph.

COPACABANA COCKTAIL

1 measure of cachaça
¾ measure of cream
¾ measure of chocolate syrup
1½ measures of papaya juice
¾ measure of pineapple juice

Combine all the ingredients in a shaker. Mix well to a Latin rhythm à la Carmen Miranda and pour into a Highball glass filled with crushed ice.

The original Copa closed for three years following the death of Monte Proser in 1973. It reopened as a discothèque in 1976 and in the following decades moved location several times. Its most recent incarnation is as a club in Times Square.

FRENCH CHAMPAGNE

'Champagne's funny stuff. I'm used to whiskey. Whiskey is a slap on the back. Champagne's a heavy mist before my eyes.' – James Stewart as Macaulay Connor in The Philadelphia Story

Champagne did not thrill Sinatra. If he chose to drink wine it was usually red, French or Italian – there were cases of Pétrus and Mouton Rothschild in the cellar of his Palm Springs home. Red wine was manly; he regarded white wine as vaguely suspect, a woman's drink. He understood that champagne signified status, and he knew that it was considered romantic, so he would order bottles to impress and delight female companions. He would sip it on the many occasions that toasts were required but usually set aside his glass immediately afterwards. Ava loved it, however, and since it was the drink that Humphrey Bogart raised to make the toast 'Here's looking at you, kid' in *Casablanca* even Sinatra could not call it sissy.

BLACK VELVET

Chilled champagne	*Half fill a large, chilled flute with*
Cold Guinness	*champagne, then very slowly top the glass*
	up with cold Guinness.

In 1861 the British nation and Empire were mourning the death of Prince Albert. Queen Victoria expressed her grief by wearing black, and many of her subjects did likewise as a mark of respect. In London the head barman at Brooks's Club decided that champagne, too, should follow suit, so he mixed sparkling wine with dark stout to produce the first Black Velvet. The cocktail's name was a reference to the black velvet ribbons worn as armbands or around hats in remembrance of Albert, but it also describes the sublime effect of the liquid as it is flows down the throat. Since both champagne and Guinness are exuberant liquids, prone to froth, it is essential to pour the drink slowly. When properly and successfully poured, champagne first, the result should be a pleasing semi-layered effect. In Germany it is often called the Bismarck, as the Iron Chancellor was known to enjoy large quantities of the drink supped from beer mugs.

A more economical version, the Poor Man's Black Velvet, is made with cider and stout. In this version the cider is poured into the stout, making it a mixed rather than layered drink.

A young Humphrey Bogart, in the days when he had vague dreams of becoming a playwright, could often be found at the 21 Club or some other rather less salubrious speakeasy-cum-nightclub with a notebook and pipe. Rather than writing, however, he was usually drinking beer, rough Martinis or, when finances allowed, more than several Black Velvets.

A dedicated drinker who usually started early, Bogart once insisted that the problem with the world was that everyone was three drinks behind.

MIMOSA

Champagne	*Chill a champagne flute. Fill it one-third*
Grand Marnier	*full with freshly squeezed orange juice, add*
Fresh orange juice	*two or more dashes of Grand Marnier, then*
	top up the glass with cold champagne.

The very first champagne cocktail may well have been the Black Velvet (equal measures of champagne and Guinness), but in the USA, just before the beginning of the twentieth century, there was a fashion for champagne cocktails that employed a sugar cube saturated with bitters and a measure of cognac. Sometimes orange bitters were used instead of Angostura, and this may have led to the creation of the Mimosa. From the mid-1920s onwards the Mimosa became one of the most popular drinks at the Ritz Hotel in Paris. It is now regarded as a classic champagne cocktail.

LEE MILLER'S FROBISHER

2 measures of gin	*Place a handful of cracked ice in a Highball*
1 dash of Angostura bitters	*glass. Add gin, bitters and lemon peel*
1 slice of lemon peel	*then fill the glass to the brim with chilled*
Cold champagne	*champagne.*

The Frobisher of the name is often identified as Sir Martin Frobisher, the Elizabethan adventurer, reformed pirate and explorer, who made three voyages to the New World to attempt to find a trade passage to India and China. He was knighted for his part in repelling the Spanish Armada. His relationship to the cocktail may be fanciful.

Elizabeth 'Lee' Miller was the famous model-turned-photographer whose work in the 1930s, 1940s and 1950s encompassed fashion shoots and war photography. She also created portraits of many of the most famous artists of the day. This recipe combined her fondness for both gin and champagne.

CHAMPAGNE COCKTAIL

1 dash of Angostura bitters	*Chill a Burgundy glass and place the sugar*
2–3 dashes of cognac	*lump inside. Add bitters, lemon twist and*
1 lemon twist	*cognac and fill the glass to the brim with*
½ sugar lump	*iced champagne.*
Chilled champagne	

The signature cocktail of Café Chambord, a New York restaurant that served French *haute cuisine*. It opened in 1936 but closed in 1964. During the 1950s it was owned by theatrical producer Harry Margolis, who often entertained actor friends such as Orson Welles and Joseph Cotton. It was Welles who once opined that there are three intolerable things in life: cold coffee, lukewarm champagne and overexcited women.

Peter Lawford, Sammy Davis Jr, Sinatra, Joey Bishop, Dean Martin, the Rat
Pack at the Sands: 'Don't think – drink!' – unless you're Joey Bishop

How Did All These People Get in My Room?

'Just a little group of ordinary guys that get together once a year to take over the entire world.' – Sammy Davis Jr

Sammy Davis was joking with the press about what at the time was probably the most famous clique in the Western world – a cohort of renowned entertainers who became known variously as the 'Summit', the 'Clan' and even the 'Jack Pack' (in honour of the fun-loving JFK, dubbed 'Chicky Boy' by Sinatra) but who are mostly remembered chiefly as the Rat Pack.

Frank, Dean, Sammy, Peter and Joey were not the original Rat Pack, but they were the most infamous. Sinatra loved company all his life. He joined a street gang as a kid and in adolescence hung out with fellow music fans. He loved drinking and talking with musicians in the Harry James and Tommy Dorsey bands, and when he began to achieve the fame he believed his talent merited he sought out fellow celebrities to carouse with.

The first Rat Pack was formed in the mid-1950s in Hollywood. In June of 1955 a group of friends that included Sinatra, Humphrey Bogart, David Niven, Mike Romanoff, Jimmy Van Heusen and Judy Garland had travelled to Vegas to attend Noël Coward's opening night at the Desert Inn. After more than a few hours of boozing Lauren Bacall, who had absented herself from much of the debauchery, spotted the survivors in a casino gaming-room and announced that the group 'looked like a goddamned rat pack'. Bacall had the measure of her friends – adults who acted like over-privileged delinquents most of the time – and a few days later, when the same group had gathered at Romanoff's, she greeted them with the words, 'I see the rat pack is all here.' They were the opposite of offended and decided to make the title official. Sinatra was particularly enthusiastic and was designated 'Pack Master'.

Everyone loved the joke. Jack Entratter of the Sands sent them all gift-wrapped white rats; they drew up a coat of arms (a rat gnawing on a hand), devised a motto ('Never rat on a rat') and ordered lapel pins in the shape of a rat's head with rubies for eyes. Several founder members were given executive positions, including Judy Garland (first Vice-President), Lauren Bacall (Den Mother) and agent Irving Paul 'Swifty' Lazar (Treasurer).

Bogart was nominated Rat in Charge of Publicity and used a newspaper interview to confirm the existence of the Holmby Hills Rat Pack. It had been formed, he told the journalist, for 'the relief of boredom and the perpetuation of independence. We admire ourselves and don't care for anybody else.' Bogart loved practical jokes, and the idea that this assemblage of friends who met regularly and enjoyed each other's company, were organized into a club with meetings, minutes and rules was ridiculous. Of course, it wasn't serious. Bogart's first reaction when the press approached him to ask about the Rat Pack was that news must be pretty tight when you start to cover parties at Romanoff's. When they insisted on knowing more he simply extended the jape. Two months after the press announcement none of the gang felt like laughing after the news that Humphrey Bogart had been diagnosed with throat cancer. The Holmby Hills Rat Pack soon ceased to be.

The second Rat Pack was different. This time Sinatra was no junior member or latecomer; he was the undisputed Leader. He handpicked the individuals who made up this merry band and gathered them together in Vegas in January 1960 to make the film *Ocean's 11* during the day and pound the stage of the Sands of an evening.

Sinatra had appeared alongside Dean Martin in Los Angeles in February 1957, just a month after Bogart died, and they performed on the same bill together three more times that year. The following year they appeared together along with Shirley MacLaine in the film *Some Came Running*, sharing an apartment and frightening the locals of Madison, Indiana, with their drunken off-screen antics (Frank was bored). Rumours of his behaviour drew a reporter from *Life* magazine. Sinatra refused to speak to him, and an article appeared in which Frank was accused of being the 'paramount chieftain' of a select group of close associates known as the 'Clan'. According to the piece, inclusion in the group was limited to those on whom Sinatra smiled. He detested the article – it described him as an angry, middle-aged man – but the Clan epithet stuck for a time. In January 1959 Dean asked his new best buddy to serve as conductor for his album *Sleep Warm*; later in the year Frank and Dean messed around together for the first time on stage at the Sands.

Dean was a natural for the show planned in Las Vegas in early 1960, as was Sammy Davis, a multi-talented performer whom Sinatra had first encountered in 1941. Comedian Joey Bishop was chosen by Frank as MC; he had known him since the early 1950s, and he had opened for Sinatra at the Copacabana. Why Peter Lawford was also invited was at first something of a mystery; he was a not particularly successful British actor who could barely sing and danced a little, although he was (mystery solved) also related to Jack Kennedy through marriage. Sinatra's preferred nomenclature for this gathering was the 'Summit', a nod to the meeting of world leaders (American, Soviet, British and French) that was scheduled for the spring of 1960. Jack Entratter sent a telegram to Sinatra, signed Khrushchev, saying, 'You come to my summit meeting and I'll come to yours.'

The four weeks on stage at the Sands attracted 34,000 paying customers. In the first week alone the hotel had to turn down 18,000 reservation requests. Regular three-dollar tickets changed hands for a hundred bucks, and members of the public fortunate enough to get in found themselves part of a crowd packed with celebrities – plus the occasional gangster. Senator Kennedy visited one night and sat ringside, joining the principals backstage after the show. The act was summed up by one columnist as 'a glorification of the American alcoholic', and this was hardly an exaggeration. Songs were attempted but hardly ever finished properly. Sammy danced, but the main focus was on the group's idea of fun – jokes about sex and boozing.

People wanted to see what Playboy described as 'the innest in-group in the world' drinking and falling over – and that was what they got. 'How did all these people get in my room?' Dean would ask as he stumbled on stage, suddenly noticing the audience. 'I gotta get me a drink,' he would announce, and when Sinatra pointed out that he was already clutching a tumbler of Scotch, he would reply, 'Oh is that my hand?' Sinatra would tell the room, 'We haven't seen much daylight since we got here. Seen a lot of Jack Daniel's but not much daylight.'

'Drinking a great deal was a prerequisite for being a Clan member,' Sammy confided to reporters. Nobody doubted him. There were rumours that some of the stuff consumed on stage was non-alcoholic, but there were several casino employees ready to swear that everybody except Joey drank, really drank, during the act. When the curtain fell they would proceed to the gaming-rooms to drink more, gamble and genially insult each other. In the mornings, before filming, they would congregate in the hotel steam-room, requisitioned as a clubhouse, and start once more. They enjoyed themselves so much that they decided to do it again and again. There were more Rat Pack films – *Sergeants Three, Four for Texas, Robin and the Seven Hoods* (which featured Sammy Cahn's ode to alcohol, 'Mr Booze') – and more appearances on stage in Miami, Atlantic City, New Jersey and Palm Springs as well as anywhere else they happened to be together and the mood took them.

Sinatra disliked the fact that the name Rat Pack had been revived, but the press – who persisted for a while longer with the classification 'Clan' – and public loved it. Journalist Richard Gehman, who wrote for *Esquire, Time, Life* and *Good Housekeeping*, published a paperback, *Sinatra and His Rat Pack*, that quickly went through three editions and established the public legend for good. Gehman hinted at insider knowledge – he was also a contributing editor at *Playboy* and had known Bogart – and the book contained a comprehensive list of first- and second-division hipsters as well as a useful dictionary of Rat Pack jargon. Sinatra, the Pack and their antics became a national obsession. Their every move was chronicled by columnists, and there was even a television debate concerning their behaviour and influence; the team defending them included Sinatra's drinking buddies Toots Shor, Jackie Gleason and Joe E. Lewis.

Sinatra seemed to have the world on a string. The Rat Pack was not simply a lounge act, albeit the biggest lounge act of all time; for a while they were the nexus of the US entertainment industry. Film and record producers catered to their every whim (in actuality *Frank's* every whim); artists that they decided were *simpatico* flourished; those they decided were square ('Harveys' in their parlance) were shut out. They also, so they thought, had the White House. Even the Leader had to have a hero, and Frank's was JFK. He directed the full force of the Rat Pack towards supporting Kennedy's election, playing benefits, hosting fund-raisers, appearing at the Democratic convention, releasing a campaign song, and he was rewarded with personal thanks and the chance to organize the new President's inaugural gala.

Chicky Boy loved showbiz gossip and beautiful, available women, and Frank supplied plenty of both. It was, however, considered increasingly unseemly for a world leader to be seen cavorting with the Clan. Sinatra saw the danger signs, and as early as the final stages of the election was issuing statements to the effect that 'There is no such entity as the Clan, and there never has been. I am fortunate to have many friends and many circles of friends, but there is no membership card.' The only organized groups to which he belonged, he insisted, were 'the various guilds that are part of my professional life'. The rest of the Pack took turns at playing down or denying the existence of an unsavoury clique.

The 1960s had not got properly under way before the Pack showed signs of collapsing under its own weight. It was Bobby Kennedy who initiated the split. In 1962 he finally managed to convince his brother to sever all connections with Sinatra, citing not just his debauched lifestyle but also his Mafia connections as potential sources of acute embarrassment to the President. Finding himself snubbed by the White House, an angry Sinatra blamed Peter Lawford and excised him from the group and from his life. Joey Bishop fell out of favour soon afterwards. In 1965 the Rat Pack (Dean, Frank and Sammy) performed their only ever televised concert with Johnny Carson standing in for Joey as MC. There was a mini-Summit at the Sands the following year, but it was, to all intents and purposes, over.

In December 1987 Sinatra, Martin and Davis were at Chasen's to announce a twenty-nine-date tour sponsored by HBO and American Express. Of course, the press dubbed it the Rat Pack reunion, but Frank berated reporters who used 'that stupid phrase' and insisted it be called the Together Again tour. Whatever it was called it rapidly descended into farce, and Dean walked.

The legend of the Rat Pack lives on today through the myriad tribute acts that appear on stages all over the world, but it's unlikely the originals would be impressed at the sight of actors and impressionists pantomiming their antics, repeating thoroughly rehearsed ad-libs *ad nauseam* and, perhaps worst of all, sipping coloured water or ginger ale as though it were Scotch.

DINO

'And now here he is, ladies and gentlemen, the star of our show. Direct from the bar . . . Mr Dean Martin.'

The abiding image of Dean Martin – debonair and vaguely soused in a tux, his easy baritone unbusied by some tune, tumbler of Scotch in one hand, a cigarette between second and third fingers. He seemed to be the personification of indolence, working only to avoid exertion of any kind. Had he been a jockey he would have won most of his races by only a short head.

'Boy, I was so loaded last night that when I fell down I missed the floor.'

At least some of this (the drunk bit?) had to be an act. A hopeless lush, no matter how amiable, could not have managed to become one of the highest-paid entertainers in the world, a superstar of music, film and television. Even Sinatra was perceived as having failed on television. Dean set a record in terms of fees for the renewal of his massively popular 1960s television show, garnering an unprecedented $283,000 per episode plus shares, so someone had acute business acumen. He also negotiated a unique clause that stipulated he was not required to attend any rehearsals. He had tapes sent to his home and would just turn up on the day.

Born 7 June 1917 in Steubenville, Ohio, Dino Crocetti was the son of immigrants Gaetano and Angela Crocetti and spoke only Italian dialect before starting school. Entirely ungifted academically, he quit school at sixteen ('because I thought I was smarter than the teacher') and worked a succession of menial jobs including shoe-shine boy, gas-station attendant and store clerk. A stint at the local steel mill convinced him that hard work was not for him. He boxed for a time under the name 'Kid Crochet' and was apparently a fairly decent amateur welterweight, but he also ruled out being hit for a living as a career choice.

During the Depression he sometimes made money delivering illegal liquor over state lines, selling lottery tickets and taking small bets. This led to a familiarity with Steubenville's gambling establishments and a

Dean Martin indulging his one true love – playing golf at the Palm Springs Golf Course in 1969

position as a croupier, where he became adept at handling cards and surreptitiously slipping silver dollars into his boots, a habit that would have earned him a severe beating at the very least if the management had become aware of it. Like the young Sinatra, he inevitably mixed with the gangster element, and although he was savvy enough at least to pretend to show the requisite respect he never revered them the way Frank seemed to.

Working (and playing) in Mob-owned establishments meant that he saw plenty of the entertainers who earned their dues there, and that gave him an idea. He began singing around the Midwest and was eventually spotted by Cleveland bandleader Ernie McKay, who made him a featured vocalist. It was McKay who suggested a name change, to Dino Martini – McKay thought that people might mistake him for, or at least presume he was related to, Nino Martini; a hugely popular opera singer of the time. By the early 1940s he was managing to acquire some dates in New York and in 1943 signed a contract to appear exclusively at the Riobamba Room. The following year he had a regular fifteen-minute radio slot on a New York station. Always eminently clubbable, he became friendly with the comedy star Lou Costello, and it was he who suggested that he have a nose job.

According to an oft-repeated story Dean borrowed the five hundred dollars for the cosmetic surgery from at least a dozen friends but spent the money elsewhere. Costello and a few others eventually put up the money again, this time paying the doctor directly and obliging Dean to turn up at the appointed time. He married for the first time in 1941. Betty Anne McDonald was, appropriately enough, the daughter of a distillery salesman. Although they had four children together he lived life like a bachelor. They argued about his late-night drinking, serial womanizing and indifference, eventually divorcing in 1949.

Undoubtedly talented but with not very much to mark him out from dozens of other Crosby copyists, Dean Martin, as he now was, might have carried on for years as a mildly successful laid-back crooner but for an impromptu pairing with a lantern-jawed comic by the name of Jerry Lewis. They had shared a bill on a couple of occasions, but around 1946 they started performing as a duo. Their act, which consisted largely of Jerry interrupting Dean's singing, became one of the most popular on the nightclub circuit, and by 1949 they had their own NBC radio show and had made the first of sixteen films together. Their stage personas – Jerry as a needy, whining, near-moron and Dean as his coolly suave buddy – were an invention but did bear some similarities to real life. Lewis's insecurity was real as was Dean's detachment. Towards the end of the relationship Dean told Jerry, 'You can talk about love all you want, but to me you're just a fucking dollar sign.'

After ten years together a parting was inevitable. Over-familiarity had soured the friendship, and both men felt trapped, Dean more so. They played their last show together at the Copacabana in July 1956. Sammy Davis sat ringside as did Jackie Gleason – Gleason jumped on stage and begged them to reconsider the split. Although he had a string of hits and a recording deal with Capitol, most insiders predicted a rapid demise for Martin. His first film after separating from Lewis, *Ten Thousand Bedrooms*, was a flop, but he acquitted himself well in two straight dramatic roles, *The Young Lions* (with Marlon Brando and Montgomery Clift) and *Some Came Running*, on which he bonded off set with Sinatra.

Sinatra and Martin became known as the 'Italian Book Ends', united by a shared love of boozing, woman-chasing and singing. They were blood brothers – Dean joked that they had pricked their thumbs to seal the pact but that Sinatra had wanted to open their wrists. 'I told him, no, that's good enough.' Temperamentally, though, they could not have been more different. Sinatra erupted frequently; Martin never lost his cool. One time when Sinatra called a hotel manager up to the room to berate him and punches started being thrown, Dean – who was comfortable in an easy chair – politely requested that the two men move to the left a little because they were blocking his view of the television.

That Dean Martin drank was beyond dispute, but just how much and how often is the subject of much debate. The pretence of being drunk on stage was, according to some commentators, first suggested by Ed Simmons, a writer on *The Colgate Comedy Hour*, which Dean hosted occasionally during the 1950s) who thought that if the audience thought Dean was tipsy he might more easily get away with some of his more outrageous asides. He was also uncomfortable with baring his emotions (in public and private), even in song. Sinatra was the obvious exception, but Dean did not approve of people in the business who performed all wrought up, making a show of putting their heart and soul into a performance. It struck him as too needy and, usually, phoney – perhaps, even, unmanly. Being drunk, or play-acting drunk, ensured that nobody would ever accuse him of taking himself too seriously. With Lewis and Martin he had his partner to interrupt him. After the split he interrupted himself.

His relationship with Frank was unique – he was the only one who ever said 'No, thanks' or 'Why?' He was also the only member of the gang who was allowed to leave early – early by Sinatra standards meant shortly before the arrival of the milkman. His usual excuse was that he had a girl waiting in his room, generally a lie. He once found a girl waiting for him in his bed. She told him Frank had paid her a thousand dollars to be there. He gave her two thousand to go back and tell Frank how good he had been. He enjoyed carousing but had other interests – golf, comics and watching television; he loved old westerns. He even called police anonymously to complain about the noise from a party at his own Beverley Hills home one night – a wedding anniversary bash. He had golf the following morning and wanted to sleep.

Shirley MacLaine, an honorary Rat Packer, described the Clan as primitive children who would put crackers in each other's beds and dump spaghetti over new tuxedos. She always had a particularly soft spot for Dean, though – not least because, in her opinion, he was the only one who acted like a grown-up. When he turned up to Sinatra's place one morning in the late 1960s to find him, Jimmy Van Heusen and Jilly Rizzo still in bed and several professional ladies in various states of undress dotted around the apartment, he surveyed the scene, sighed and wondered out loud, 'Jesus, don't they ever get sick of this shit?' Late in life it was Dean, of all people, who occasionally voiced some regret at the Rat Pack's antics, admitting that 'we coulda been nicer to each other and to the dames. Especially the dames.'

Few people, however, had a bad word for him. Everybody loved him. He was effortlessly stylish, charismatic and funny. But even his longest friendships did not run deep, and he gave little of himself away. Sammy Davis told *People* magazine in 1988, 'I don't think Dean ever did two and half pages of conversation in his life.' Jeanne Martin, who was married to him for twenty-three years and to whom he remained close after their divorce, described family mealtimes during their marriage. 'Dean wasn't much for chit-chat. So I'd put the television behind me where he could see it, and we'd all sit there and watch while we ate.'

His air of detachment projected an aura of laconic cool, but in his later years he became more of a taciturn loner, almost a recluse. By 1980 he had more or less unofficially retired from performing and was spending his days playing golf at the Riviera Country Club in Pacific Palisades, his nights eating out at his favourite Italian restaurant, La Famiglia. He would arrive at 7.30, alone, drink two or three Scotch Rocks and order spaghetti with tomato and fresh basil then tiramisu for dessert. (He sometimes removed his dentures when he ate and placed them on the table next to him.) Afterwards he went home to try to catch a western on television and then go to bed.

He disappeared even more into himself after the death of his beloved son, Dean Paul, in 1987. A pilot in the California National Guard, Dean Paul's F-4C Phantom jet collided with a mountain during a training exercise. His father was utterly devastated, and those who knew him believed he never really recovered. Part of the reason Sinatra was determined to perform the 1988 Together Again tour was that he was convinced it would help occupy his friend, distract him from his grief. He should have paid more attention to Dean when he suggested, 'Why don't we find a good bar instead?' After only six dates, Dean yelled 'I wanna go home' from the stage and flicked a lit cigarette at the audience. Sinatra eventually lost patience with him and tipped a plate of spaghetti over his head. Dean flew back to Los Angeles and checked into a hospital alleging kidney trouble. He appeared fine a few days later when he quipped, 'Frank sent me a kidney, but I don't know whose it was.'

In his final years his health began to fail him. He tried to cut back on the smoking and drinking, but it was way, way too late. When La Famiglia closed in 1995 he switched venues to another Beverley Hills Italian restaurant, Da Vinci's, where he would order the same meal and drinks every night. I'm just waiting to die, he told Paul Anka one night. Two weeks before his death he stopped eating. He passed away on Christmas Day 1995 of acute respiratory failure brought on by emphysema. It was well known that Sinatra never forgave, but a few weeks before Dean's death they had a reconciliation of sorts over a meal. They laughed and ended up throwing bread rolls at each other. After he was gone Sinatra mourned and promised that there would always be a place in his heart and soul for Dean.

SCOTCH ROCKS

1 large measure of J&B Scotch Ice cubes 1 book of matches 1 cigarette	*Drop two or three ice cubes in a tumbler and pour the Scotch over them. Light a cigarette.*

He sipped a lot of fancy drinks in his lifetime, but classic Scotch on the Rocks was a constant. Immaculately stylish, suave, urbane and unperturbed, admired by armies of men and desired by hosts of women, Dean Martin at his best was one of the very few individuals who could be as witty while drinking as most people *think* they are when drunk.

SAMMY

The Wham of Sam!

He was hectic, always moving, barely ever still, possessed of a seemingly inexhaustible energy, fuelled partly by self-belief (although even Sammy had his insecurities) and a determination to get back at (and silence, however briefly) the hateful racists and bigots who tried to make him suffer. He fought against them with the best weapon he had: his talent. He sang, played trumpet, drums, piano, vibraphone, danced, acted, wrote – forty albums, countless film and television performances, standing ovations and record-breaking runs on Broadway. He was Sammy Davis Jr, and he wanted to be the greatest entertainer in the world. 'I gotta get bigger,' he would demand of himself when he looked in the mirror. 'I gotta get bigger.'

Entering the world on 8 December 1925, Sammy Davis might as well have been born in a trunk. His mother was a tap-dancing chorus girl, his father a seasoned vaudevillian. They separated soon after Sammy's arrival, and he was initially raised by his maternal grandmother, Rosa. By the age of three he was on the road with his father, Big Sam, and Will Mastin. They played the African-American vaudeville theatres and burlesque houses, the so-called 'Chitlin' Circuit', often barely earning enough to eat properly – such venues paying even less than the white-audience theatres at a time when vaudeville was being decimated by talking pictures and radio.

Young Sammy watched his father at work, watched all the acts from the side of the stage and started acting out his own versions of the routines he saw. He was a natural, and Mastin and Big Sam realized he might even make a novelty addition to their act. Disguising the toddler with fake whiskers and billing him as 'Silent Sam the Dancing Midget' had the added advantage of misdirecting the child-welfare authorities – consequently Sammy had little in the way of formal education. He eventually graduated from special billing – 'Will Mastin's Gang featuring Little Sammy' – to becoming a fully fledged part of the Will Mastin Trio.

Sammy Davis idolized Sinatra. They first met in 1941 when the Mastin Trio were booked as a last-minute opening act for the Tommy Dorsey Band. Davis was approached backstage by a young white man who shook his hand and said, 'My name's Frank. I sing with Dorsey.' During their three weeks together, Sinatra would call in on him in his dressing-room, and they would swap stories.

For Davis this was unprecedented – 'the average top vocalist in those days wouldn't give the time of day to a Negro supporting act', he said when recalling the dates. Not long after this he was drafted into the army, where he suffered horrendous racist bullying. He was unofficially segregated from the white troops, almost tricked into drinking a beer bottle full of urine (it was then poured over his head); he had his nose broken twice and was held down while the word 'coon' was daubed on his face in whitewash. What saved him from this and worse was being asked by an officer to help create a touring production for entertaining servicemen across the country. He spent the final eight months of his service on the road visiting other military training camps, avoiding the worst of the institutionalized bigotry by virtue of his skills at entertaining.

After the war Davis greeted Sinatra outside a radio station in Hollywood. Sammy was still in uniform. Frank remembered him and made sure he got tickets to the show. He remembered him again when he was playing in New York in 1947 and made the Will Mastin Trio his supporting act, insisting on a fee that was three times their normal payment. At the end of the run they were officially friends, signalled by the fact that Sinatra's parting words were those he reserved for the people he felt close to: 'Anybody hits you, you let me know.'

By the early 1950s the Trio was one of the hottest acts on any circuit, and Sam was absolutely the star of the show. As well as the dancing he sang, did comic turns and impressions of white stars – Jimmy Cagney, Humphrey Bogart, Cary Grant, even Frank Sinatra. The act became his showcase, and he began gaining solo prominence with recordings (he signed to Decca in 1954) and appearances on radio and television.

In 1951 they opened at Ciro's on Sunset Strip, and the audience was packed out with Hollywood stars. They were a huge smash again at the Copacabana in New York. Despite being the toast of both towns there were still places where a black man was not welcome as a paying customer. Sinatra kept in touch, sending congratulatory telegrams and encouraging Sammy to keep on banging on doors, breaking barriers. In 1954, when he was playing the Apollo, he invited Ava Gardner to attend the show. She turned up, took a bow on stage and posed with him for publicity shots. This was a major Hollywood star – more significantly a white Southern lady – on stage at the Apollo. He was making progress. The Will Mastin Trio had played Vegas before, a residency at the Last Frontier hotel and casino in the mid-1940s, but after Sammy finished dazzling the audience on stage he had not been allowed to enter, or even see, the casino.

A decade later he was invited back to Vegas, headlining at the same hotel, being paid $7,500 a week and, most importantly, being allowed full access to the restaurant, bar and gaming tables. It was a massive vindication and triumph, the only drawback was that he had recording commitments and would have to commute between LA and Vegas. It was a small inconvenience; but then one night in November 1954, driving back to LA, he swerved into oncoming traffic while trying to avoid a car in front of him that suddenly attempted a U-turn. He almost lost his life; he did lose his left eye, punctured and destroyed on impact with the horn button on the steering wheel. Frank visited him in hospital, and when he was released he took him into his Palm Springs house to recuperate, then they spent Christmas in New Jersey with Sinatra's parents. When he was well enough Frank helped him find a new place to live, all the time urging Sammy to start performing again.

His first gig after the accident was at Ciro's, supporting Janis Paige. Paige had a clause written into her contract that the opening act should take no more than two bows. The first night Sammy stormed the place, and the Trio received eight bows. The management decided to reverse the billing, and Paige became the support act.

Sammy now worshipped Frank, at least to the extent that Frank had Bogart. He copied his gait; he wore the same hats, positioned at the same jaunty angle; when Frank took to wearing white raincoats so did Sammy. Frank returned some of this devotion by talking in public about Sammy's awesome talent and even adopting some of Sammy's finger-clicking, jazzy singing style. Now he seemed unstoppable. In 1956 he made his Broadway début in *Mr Wonderful* (which ran for over 400 performances and gave him the hit single 'Too Close for Comfort'); in 1958 he played Sportin' Life in the film version of *Porgy and Bess*; in 1959 he was one of the stars of *The Big Party*, a lavish CBS television variety show. He was a celebrity. Everyone knew Sammy – tight sharkskin suit, heavy jewellery around his neck and fingers – a showbiz dynamo. Celebrity was occasionally dangerous for someone like him, however – his public conversion to Judaism caused much comment as did his well-known fondness for squiring beautiful white women.

In 1957 studio bosses panicked at the potential scandal that might erupt when he began an affair with Kim Novak. Sammy received a visit in his dressing-room from a gun-wielding mobster who threatened to put out his other eye if he didn't stop seeing the white girl. Mixed-race relationships were still taboo at the time, and he was forced into a sham marriage with a young black dancer he hardly knew. That lasted a year.

Sinatra, his hero, sanctified him by making him a member of the Rat Pack – he did not like the name Clan; too many obvious connotations for a man of his hue – making possible an even more triumphant return to Vegas than the one that the accident had curtailed. Yet, despite everything he felt he owed Sinatra, some things still rankled. There were jokes at his expense on stage (but then again there were jokes at everyone's expense on stage), and there was, despite Sinatra's liberal sensibilities, an underlying lazy, casual racism apparent in the group. He didn't object to his nickname, 'Smokey', because it referred to his chain-smoking habit rather than his skin colour, but he disliked being referred to as jungle bunny or being introduced as 'the little black boy who will sing for us'. Making him wear a brown robe and handing him a bar of brown soap in the steam-room of the Sands, when everyone else present had white monogrammed bathrobes and ivory soap, was another one of the small, unthinking cruelties that, he admitted years later, did hurt. He knew it was never vindictive, but Frank's idea of a harmless joke sometimes caused pain. Still it was Sinatra who put an arm around him to console him and told him to ignore the Southern State delegates who booed him when the Pack played a Democrat convention, and it was Frank who refused to play or stay at any place that wouldn't take Sammy.

Being close to Sinatra inevitably meant witnessing the occasional outburst of venom, and Sammy was a little too candid about this during a radio interview in Chicago that was picked up by all the media. He began well, praising the Leader as 'the kindest man in the world to me when I lost my eye and wanted to die'. There was a 'but', however, a large one. 'But there are many things he does that there are no excuses for,' he continued. 'Talent is not an excuse for bad manners. I don't care if you are the most talented person in the world. It does not give you the right to step on people and treat them rotten. This is what he does occasionally.' Sinatra was apoplectic and cut Davis off completely. He refused to see him and had his part in a new movie written out. Sammy was beside himself. Sinatra let him suffer for a few months then allowed him to apologize in public before being accepted back into the fold. Sammy counted himself lucky.

Post-Rat Pack he established himself on Broadway once more, earning a Tony nomination for 1964's *Golden Boy*. By 1966 he had his own weekly television show, and he made more television appearances, had more film roles and hit records throughout that decade and well beyond. Inevitably, however, somebody who had been as hip and happening as Sammy was in the late 1950s and 1960s eventually becomes stale, precisely because he was so of the moment. In 1975 he was given his own chat show, but it was short-lived – for once his energy levels worked against him, as viewers could not take to a host who had difficulty sitting back and letting others perform. He would never fade totally from view, and he was a welcome guest on everything from *The Tonight Show* to *The Cosby Show* and appeared on the daytime soap *One Life to Live* several times between 1979 and 1983. In 1990 *Sammy Davis Jr's 60th Anniversary Celebration* won an Emmy for Outstanding Variety, Musical or Comedy Special. When Frank decided they should get back together in the late

1980s Sammy was, of course, all for it – they even rehearsed at his house. Unlike Dean he stayed the course and was something like his old self.

Sammy Davis lived a life of compulsive vitality, always striving to be the best and taking everything at full tilt. The downside of this was an addictive personality, hardly capable of restraint. He drank, smoked and spent to excess. He earned and spent fortunes – $50 million gone over a twenty-year period by his own estimation – and despite his success he usually had financial worries. At one point, when his outgoings were coming close to eclipsing his income, he found a new accountant and asked what he should do. The man told him he *had* to curb his spending – no more extravagances; stick to a budget. Sammy listened, nodded, agreed with everything he had to say. The next day the accountant received a package, a solid-gold Cartier cigarette case with an inscription, 'Thanks for the advice. Sammy.' The drinking and smoking were also addictions he struggled with, and his body suffered. After everything he went through there was one last trial – months of pain, chemotherapy, radiation treatment and grief from the IRS. He died of throat cancer in May 1990.

Sinatra had visited him repeatedly in hospital, putting on a brave face for Sammy's sake but breaking down in tears after leaving. He was buried wearing the gold wristwatch Frank had presented him with after their final tour. Throat cancer was the same disease that killed Bogart. It had been Bogart who, a year after the accident, had persuaded Sammy to lose the eye-patch. He had grown use to it, even convinced himself that it lent him a rakish air, but the truth was he had been afraid to take it off in public. Bogart called him on it, asked him if he wanted to be remembered as Sammy Davis Jr or the entertainer with the eye-patch. He pulled it off on stage one night soon after. The audience was initially stunned into silence but then stood up and applauded.

And people do remember Sammy Davis Jr.

SALTY DOG

1 measure of chilled vodka

Fresh grapefruit juice

Wet the rim of a Highball glass with fresh grapefruit juice and dip it in salt. Add chilled vodka and grapefruit juice to a cocktail shaker with a handful of ice cubes. Shake well and strain into the prepared glass.

Not strictly speaking a hangover cure, but Sammy, when he was busy, as he almost always was, was fond of invigorating himself with one (or maybe two) Salty Dogs first thing in the morning. Piratical eye-patch optional.

PETER

Brother-in-Lawford

Peter Lawford described himself as 'a halfway decent-looking English boy who looked nice in a drawing-room standing by a piano'. It was a fairly accurate description. Talent-wise he was small beer, but the apparent veneer of English sophistication served him well in Hollywood. His mother, May Somerville Bunny, was a monster – a warped, grotesque, controlling megalomaniac whose behaviour encouraged her first husband to shoot himself in the head. She titled her own memoir *Bitch!* Her second husband, a British Army surgeon, was not present at Peter's birth in London in 1923, as he was certain the child was not his. The couple had been living apart after many years of marital strife. Peter's father was actually her husband's commanding officer, Sir Sydney Lawford, a married man and war hero who had earned his knighthood during the First World War and who was known by fellow officers as 'Swanky Syd'. Peter's parentage was an open secret, and shortly after his birth divorce petitions were filed. Lawford did the decent thing, marrying May and giving Peter his name.

Although Peter's arrival allowed May to become Lady May, a title she delighted in and insisted others always use, she regarded the child as a nuisance. She had been thirty-eight when she fell pregnant, and the birth had been a great inconvenience to her. Peter was a large baby and caused her excruciating pain. She would also have preferred him to have been a girl, so she dressed him in pink for several years. The scandal surrounding his birth meant that she had no opportunity to enjoy her new title in London; the couple were ostracized and forced to flee the country. They led a peripatetic existence, passing through Europe, Australia, Brazil, India, South America, the South Pacific, living in such places as Monte Carlo, Ceylon, Tahiti, Hawaii and California. It was in Hawaii that Peter first discovered surfing, a life-long passion.

Although May dictated a strict health regime and organic diet for the boy – any type of sweet was prohibited – she had little real interest in his

The 'brother-in-Lawford', 'a halfway decent-
looking English boy who looked nice in a
drawing-room standing by a piano'

upbringing and put him in the care of nurses and servants. His education was overseen by a succession of tutors and governesses – at least one of whom apparently sexually abused him – and his lack of formal education embarrassed him in later life. In early childhood he managed only broken English but became fluent in French, Spanish and German. He lacked any playmates of his own age, which led to a certain precocity – he was brought out at social functions and expected to entertain the grown-ups. May had always been keen on amateur dramatics and was delighted when Peter had small parts in two films, the first in Britain when he was eight and the second in Hollywood shortly afterwards. However, General Lawford was horrified that any son of his should become an actor and put a stop to the whole business. When Peter was old enough he told Sir Sydney he would not follow him into the military and, accompanied by May, returned to Hollywood. After a few years struggling with bit parts, in 1943 he signed a contract with MGM.

It was at an MGM party in 1944 that the 21-year-old Peter first met Frank, who had recently moved to Hollywood and signed his own five-year contract. Two years later they worked together for the first time on the film *It Happened in Brooklyn* – Peter, naturally, playing a British aristocrat. They began socializing. Frank held New Year's Eve parties at his Hollywood home, lavish affairs that centred on a musical-and-comedy review performed by Frank and his friends. Although it was staged in the living-room there were costumes (borrowed from MGM), props and scenery, a script. The music was written by Jule Styne, lyrics by Sammy Cahn, and the songs were mostly skits full of in-jokes. One sketch featured Frank as a waiter in a restaurant where Sammy Cahn, Peter Lawford and Harry Crane, who wrote many of the skits, were eating. Finishing the meal, Peter signalled Frank – 'Hey, waiter, I'll take the cheque now.' That was the signal for Frank to drop a full tray of dishes in shock. The routine was making fun of the fact that Peter *never* paid a tab – his tight-fistedness was legendary among friends.

Peter fell under Sinatra's spell much as Sammy had. He was in awe of him and, like Sammy, he made efforts to emulate much of his hero's style. Their friendship ended abruptly, however, in 1954 when, during one of Ava's and Frank's many splits, the press reported that Lawford had been spotted sharing an intimate dinner with Gardner. Lawford had cut quite a swathe through Hollywood starlets and leading ladies – he had an eight-month affair with Lana Turner before being dropped in favour of the drummer and bandleader Gene Krupa – and at one point had had a short fling with Ava. He was a renowned ladies' man, even though he was also dogged by rumours that the English pretty boy was gay. (It probably didn't help that May, following one particularly vicious argument with Peter, had sought revenge by barging into the office of one of the MGM studio bosses and announcing that her son was a homosexual.)

His night out with Ava, though, had been innocent. His manager had been present during the meal; nothing had happened. When he received an angry, threatening phone call from Sinatra Peter panicked and asked Jimmy Van Heusen to intervene and calm Frank down. Sinatra refused to speak to him for three years, then, in 1957, they met at a dinner party and Frank resumed the friendship as though there had never been a rift. What helped Peter was the fact that he had recently married Patricia Kennedy, a sister of John F. Kennedy. Pretty soon they were seriously socializing, getting drunk together on trips to England, Monaco and Rome. They even became partners in a restaurant business. Lawford was back in favour.

His career was also relatively healthy. As well as films he was having success in television. In 1957 he was offered the lead role in a television series based on the *Thin Man* films. He accepted, but the following year he turned down the chance of a five-picture deal with Cubby Broccoli to play James Bond. His fee would have been $25,000, and at the time he could get $75,000 per film. The role went to Sean Connery instead.

'Don't forget I've got Lawford, and remember who Lawford's got.' This was Sinatra's boast and the main reason for Peter's invitation to join the Rat Pack. Years later Lawford was blunt concerning his role in the Clan. 'I was Frank's pimp, and Frank pimped for Jack.'

Everybody knew he hadn't really earned a place on stage at the Sands. He could dance a little, but they had Sammy for that and he was in a whole different league. He could just about hold a tune, but compared with Frank or Dean . . . ? His innate English sophistication, at least as perceived in America, probably lent a touch of class to the ensemble. But he was there mainly because he was the 'Brother-in-Lawford'. And so, when Frank was humiliated by Kennedy's eventual rejection of his friendship, it was Peter who had to suffer. Sinatra could never bring himself to say anything negative about JFK himself, although he did curse Bobby, and he refused to accept that his own Mob connections had made it impossible for Kennedy to continue a friendship, so he vented all of his anger on Lawford.

Peter tried desperately to contact Frank but found himself cut off. He was ejected from the Pack, written out of future film projects and pointedly ignored by Sinatra's friends and associates. Letters and phone calls went unanswered. He asked friends to intervene. He sent his manager to meet Sinatra and make amends. Nothing worked.

Over a dozen years after the event he flew to Vegas to watch Frank at Caesar's Palace, hoping enough time had elapsed for Sinatra to consider a reconciliation. Sitting at his table with a drink he was approached by representatives of the management who informed him that unless he left Frank would not be performing. By that time he was in terminal decline. Pat had divorced him in late 1965, and he had alienated the rest of the Kennedys by turning up at Bobby's funeral with a young conquest dressed in a black micro-skirt. His film work dried up, and he was reduced to appearances on television game shows. He drank heavily and got into drugs – cannabis, pills, cocaine. When Sammy had a coke problem Sinatra ordered him to stop, and he did. Peter's friends staged an intervention and put him in the Betty Ford Clinic.

It didn't save him. His liver and kidneys were shot, he passed away on Christmas Eve 1984 at Cedars-Sinai Medical Center in Los Angeles. He had become a US citizen in 1960 so he could vote for his brother-in-law. His ashes were scattered into the Pacific Ocean.

BELLINI

2 measures of fresh peach juice or peach schnapps Chilled champagne 1 dash of raspberry or cherry liqueur	*Pour the fresh peach juice or schnapps into a chilled champagne flute. Slowly top up the glass with chilled champagne, add the liqueur, stir very carefully and serve.*

The Italian tradition of serving peaches in wine was part of the inspiration for the cocktail originated in the early 1940s by Giuseppe Cipriani, founder of Harry's Bar in Venice. Cipriani's Bellini was made using a purée of white peaches and the Italian sparkling wine prosecco. Raspberry or cherry juice was added to create a distinctive pink hue that Cipriani had seen in the work of the fifteenth-century Venetian painter Giovanni Bellini, in whose honour the drink was named. The cocktail soon became popular in the American Harry's, and champagne was deemed a more than acceptable substitute for prosecco. Fresh peach juice, or peach liqueur, or schnapps, is also commonly used in place of a purée, which is prepared by peeling and pitting white peaches then blending in a food processor.

Peter Lawford was no stranger to champagne, and he sipped it at his last evening out, a dinner with Elizabeth Taylor, the day before he collapsed and was hospitalized for the final time.

JOEY

'I was told to come here.'

At a Friars Club dinner held to honour Dean Martin, the usual group of celebrity friends and entertainers had taken turns to declare how happy, thrilled and privileged they felt at being asked to attend. The first thing Joey Bishop said when he stood up to speak was 'I was told to come here.' It got a big laugh. It was probably a spur-of-the-moment gag; many of Bishop's best jokes were. There was the time he was the support act to Sinatra at the Copacabana in 1954. He had already started his act when Marilyn Monroe arrived late, looking stunning in a white ermine coat, and naturally all eyes turned away from the stage to ogle her. Bishop waited until she was seated then barked out, 'Marilyn, I thought I told you to wait in the truck.' It brought the house down.

During the same run he was coming off stage one night when Sinatra, about to go on, asked him, 'How's the crowd tonight?'

'Great for me,' said Joey, 'but for you I don't know.'

Joseph Abraham Gottlieb was born on 3 February 1918 in the Bronx, the youngest of five children. His father was a mechanic, and the family relocated to South Philadelphia when Joey was just a few months old for his father to open a shop selling and repairing bicycles. His father played the ocarina and taught Joey Yiddish songs, but there was no show-business tradition in the family. From an early age, however, Joey had a yearning to be an entertainer. He learned to tap-dance and taught himself mandolin and banjo. He completed only two years of high school before it was thought best that he quit to help out in the family business.

He wanted to try his luck in New York, and his parents agreed to let him go on the condition that he lived with relatives in Manhattan and kept a sensible day job. He got work in a hat factory and wangled a spot as an MC at a Chinese restaurant on Broadway in the evening. His first attempt at the big time failed, so he returned to Philly and became part of a comedy-dancing act that called itself the Bishop Brothers (Joey and two non-siblings). In the late 1930s the trio got a break when spotted by club owner Frank Palumbo, who gave them a residency at his nightspot Palumbo's, where Jimmy Durante had started out.

They had another residency at the Havana Casino in Buffalo and ended up in Miami as a duo, working almost two years at the Nut Club. It was in Miami that Joey met his future wife, Sylvia Ruzga. When his comedy partner was drafted in 1941 Joey decided to go it alone, opening at the exotically named El Dumpo in Cleveland. Then he was drafted. He was in for three and a half years, achieving the rank of sergeant and becoming a recreation director. Coming out of the service he managed to extend a one-week gig at the Greenwich Village Inn to an eleven-week residency but struggled to find anything after that ended. Now married, he tried working the clubs in Sylvia's hometown of Chicago and after two years graduated to being a $1,000 a week headliner at the Chez Paree. It was 1949, and he still wanted to make it big in New York.

Finally, in 1952, he got rave reviews playing at the Latin Quarter where he was spotted by Frank Sinatra. Frank thought Joey would be a great opener for any New York shows and offered him spots at the Paramount, the Riviera and the Copa. He liked Joey so much that he also occasionally took him out on the road with him. Sinatra didn't exactly pluck him out of obscurity, but having Frank's good opinion didn't hurt.

He now had a signature look – a close-cropped haircut which he thought somehow made the jokes funnier – and a catchphrase, 'son of a gun'. He developed a style that suited his temperament – cynical, world-weary, jaded – making comments and quips rather than traditional jokes. He had a dry wit and never attempted to ingratiate himself with the audience – in fact, he often gave the impression he found it slightly degrading being forced to entertain a crowd. By 1958 he could make in the region of $200,000 a year through nightclub fees but decided to concentrate on trying to break into television and film. He managed to become a regular on a CBS panel show and was championed by legendary chat-show host Jack Parr.

On the big screen he had straight dramatic roles in three war movies, including *The Naked and the Dead* – 'I played both parts,' he would deadpan. The same year he played the Sands in a solo show. One night somebody interrupted his act about halfway through and complained loudly, 'I'm going home. You're too funny – and too young.' It was Jack Benny, Joey's all-time comedy hero. Benny was also performing in Vegas and told his own audiences to and go and see 'the funniest young comic in the business.'

As with Peter Lawford, people sometimes questioned why he was there on stage with Dean, Frank and Sammy, but Sinatra called him 'the hub of the big wheel'. Joey fulfilled a dual role. Despite the fact that he was the only professional funny man in the group it was Joey who remained mostly straight-faced while the rest of the boys clowned around. It suited his stage persona. He was the 'Frown Prince of Comedy', downbeat, deadpan, lugubrious. He was the official MC. He kept in the background and, through dint of being sober, was able to keep an eye on the time. If the others were enjoying themselves too much he could help move the show along.

The Pack were contracted to play for one hour per show, but, of course, everybody wanted more. The casino bosses knew that every extra minute spent laughing at the Pack meant customers being away from the tables, which meant less revenue. Joey's other main function was to come up with a lot of the comic stuff, write routines and patter, provide suggestions for ad-libs for those who weren't as naturally funny as himself and Dean. After JFK won the presidency Joey's title in the Jack Pack was 'Speaker of the House'.

He wrote a little skit in which Peter Lawford had to dress as a busboy and wander through the audience collecting glasses. When the spotlight picked him up, he would say, 'Imagine what I'd be doing if he didn't get elected.' It got laughs, but Bishop thought it should get more and suggested to Lawford he should place more emphasis on the word 'didn't'.

Lawford was indignant that a club comic tried to direct him – a movie star. 'Don't', he insisted, 'try to tell me how to deliver a line.'

Sinatra told Lawford, 'Deliver the line the way Joey's telling you or get the fuck out of the show.'

He took getting laughs more seriously than any of the others, but there was something else that marked him out as different. His sobriety. His only real vice was golf. 'I never had a drop of liquor in my life,' he said, 'apart from Passover wine.' He was, in his own words a 'go-homer'. Late-night partying held no allure for him. 'When we were doing the Summit Meeting shows in Vegas,' he admitted, 'the other guys would stay up until all hours, but I went to bed. I may rub elbows, but I don't raise them.' Perhaps it was this that ultimately led to his exclusion from the group. Or perhaps he made one joke too many.

Although Frank seemed to love it when he cracked wise – 'Mr Sinatra will now speak of some of the good things the Mafia has done' – there was the very real possibility that he might have caught the Leader in the wrong mood and have been perceived to have overstepped the mark. He was a complainer, and another rumour was that he found fault with his accommodation while playing at one of the casinos. Or he had deliberately failed to obey an order. When Sinatra had a brief personal feud with one club owner, and his place was boycotted, Joey apparently went there anyway. He loved Sinatra, and he loved being in the Rat Pack, but he refused to be bullied by anyone.

Whatever the reason, towards the end of 1963 he found himself written out of the new Pack film *Robin and the Seven Hoods*. He did not speak to Frank for about a year, and although he was back briefly for the mini-Summit at the Sands in 1966, the same year he had a part in one of Dean's comedy westerns, that was it for Joey and the Rat Pack. He never made a big thing of it. There seemed never to have been a dramatic falling-out, neither was there any panicky grovelling on Joey's part. Unlike Peter Lawford, or even Sammy when he was briefly banished, Joey did not ever think he would wither and die without Sinatra.

He had his own television show, a sitcom where he played a fictional talk-show host. It ran only until 1965, but in 1967 he was given an actual late-night talk show that ABC hoped would rival Johnny Carson's *Tonight Show*. The fact that it was cancelled early did not seem to bother him unduly; the pay-out for his contract was supposedly over a million. After struggling so hard for so long some people thought he gave up too quickly. He was a guest presenter for Johnny Carson a record 177 times but always insisted he was not looking for a show of his own. He made a move to Miami, content to make regular appearances on quiz and panel shows, do the occasional club date and spend his days fishing and golfing. He died in October 2007, aged eighty-nine, the last of the Pack to go.

He was proud of the time he spent alongside Frank, Dean, Sammy and Peter but was always aware of his relative status. He joked that he would call his memoirs *I Was a Mouse in the Rat Pack* (and a 2002 biography used the title), but he also pointed out that 'even the mascot gets to carry the ball, too'.

ROY ROGERS

1 small bottle of cola	*Pour the cola into a Collins glass filled with*
1 dash of grenadine	*ice. Add grenadine to taste and garnish*
1 maraschino cherry	*with the cherry.*

Clean-living singing cowboy Roy Rogers was famous enough to merit his very own non-alcoholic cocktail. Together with his wife Dale Evans – 'Queen of the West' to his 'King of the Cowboys' – his golden palomino Trigger and his faithful dog Bullet, Rogers appeared in over a hundred films. He was also a star of radio and television and had a string of hit songs including 'Cold Water', 'Tumbling Tumbleweeds' and 'Hold That Critter Down'.

As a non-drinker Joey's choices were limited, but this drink is at least more manly than the Shirley Temple, the alcohol-free cocktail created at Chasen's during the 1930s for Temple when she was a child star.

THE SANDS

Sinatra was a regular visitor to Las Vegas and early casino resorts such as the Last Frontier, El Rancho Vegas and the Flamingo, but it was not until 1951 that he appeared there as a performer. He was at a career and personal low point, and his residency at the Desert Inn was seen as a favour granted by the owner Wilbur Clark. While he was there work was going on building a new resort situated between the Desert Inn and the Flamingo. It was to be called the Sands. It opened in 1952 and was at the beginning a relatively modest enterprise with just a small casino and two hundred rooms, but it would eventually become the most famous venue in Vegas.

Billed as 'A Place in the Sun', the Sands aimed to attract a more sophisticated crowd, modelling itself, in part, on New York's Copacabana. As well as importing the Copa's famous Chinese menu it also acquired its legendary assistant manager, Jack Entratter. Entratter had been a bouncer at the Stork Club before moving to the Copacabana in 1940. He was there for twelve years and was well liked by showgirls and visiting acts, always ensuring high salaries and luxurious facilities. 'He was our love,' said Jerry Lewis. 'We wouldn't go anywhere in Vegas but where Jack was.' And so the stars flocked to play Entratter's new showroom, called – what else? – the Copa Room. Sinatra played as soon as he was free from the Desert Inn, Martin and Lewis soon after that, then Nat King Cole, Lena Horne, Tony Bennett, Louis Armstrong. The Copa Room would eventually host the Rat Pack, Count Basie, Marlene Dietrich, Ella Fitzgerald, Judy Garland, Peggy Lee, Bobby Darin, Rosemary Clooney, Wayne Newton, all America's top musical names. Frank, Dean and Sammy all recorded albums there. Dean's was titled *Live at the Sands Hotel: An Evening of Music, Laughter and Hard Liquor*.

The other great human asset for the Sands was casino manager Carl Cohen. Cohen had been running the casino at

El Ranch Vegas successfully for several years, but one night in 1955 he had a serious difference of opinion with his boss, Beldon Kavelman. Kavelman had spotted a man in jeans and tennis shoes on the casino floor and instructed Cohen to eject the undesirable. Cohen refused, an argument ensued, and Cohen, retaliating to a punch thrown by Kavelman, floored his boss with a right cross to the chin and walked out. The shabby gambler had been Howard Hughes. The following morning Cohen was offered the role at the Sands.

Kavelman was not a popular man, and Cohen was swiftly able to expand the gambling operation by offering jobs to several dealers who had also walked out of El Rancho after witnessing his departure. He also brought with him several high-rollers, including Howard Hughes. (Hughes was so grateful he would actually go on to buy the Sands some years later.)

Entratter and Cohen were a formidable team, and the Sands prospered. Its greatest moment would come towards the end of 1959 when Frank Sinatra and his friends arrived to make a film and spend their evenings playing a historic gig they would call the Summit.

The Sands was demolished in November 1996.

ATOMIC COCKTAIL

1½ measures of vodka
1½ measures of cognac
½ measure of dry sherry
1 orange wedge
Champagne

Add the vodka, cognac and sherry to a shaker filled with ice cubes. Shake well and strain into a chilled Martini glass. Top up with chilled champagne, garnish with the orange wedge and present.

The US government began atmospheric nuclear tests in the Nevada Desert in January 1951. The site was just sixty-five miles from the Strip, and the tests brought tourists. Casinos and resorts offered a range of atomic-inspired novelties, including the Atomic Hairdo, a mushroom-cloud-shaped creation styled by GeeGee, hairdresser at the Flamingo. As well as sponsoring a Miss Atomic Bomb Contest, the Sands developed its own Atomic Cocktail. Drinking more than several of these was almost certain to result in a personal implosion.

The 'Italian Book Ends' – Sinatra and Martin do their thing

Last Word

The Sands, late at night, and both audience and performers are joyfully partaking of what is generally regarded as a 'mothery gas', what US journalist James Wolcott described as 'the Mount Rushmore of men having fun'.

The Leader slows down the action in order to mock-berate his second-in-command. The patter goes as follows:

> FRANK: Say, I'd like to talk to you for a few minutes.
>
> DEAN: Why, am I in town?
>
> FRANK: Listen, I wanna talk to you about your drinking.
>
> DEAN: What happened? I miss a round?
>
> FRANK: No, you didn't miss a round. I wanna talk to you about the amount you drink.
> You know what they're saying about you?
>
> DEAN: And how about you?
>
> FRANK: Me?
>
> DEAN: Yeah, you. You shoot a pretty good stick with that bottle yourself.
>
> FRANK: Ah, but I don't inhale

Ah, but he surely did.

'Smoking is stupid,' Sinatra once insisted, but he never really gave up. Dean Martin would quip about his own smoking, saying, 'I quit every night.'

FURTHER READING

Some books that illuminate, entertain and inform

Barnes, Ken, *Sinatra and the Great Song Stylists*, Shepperton, Middlesex: Ian Allan, 1972

Friedwald, Will, *Sinatra!: The Song Is You*, New York: Scribner, 1995

Hamill, Pete, *Why Sinatra Matters,* New York: Little, Brown, 1998

Jacobs, George, and William Stadiem, *Mr S: The Last Word on Frank Sinatra*, London: Sidgwick and Jackson, 2003

Kelley, Kitty, *His Way: The Unauthorized Biography of Frank Sinatra*, New York: Bantam Press, 1986

Lahr, John, *Sinatra: The Artist and the Man*, New York: Random House, 1997

Levy, Shawn, *Rat Pack Confidential*, London: Fourth Estate, 2002

Petkov, Steven, and Leonard Mustazza (eds), *The Frank Sinatra Reader*, New York: Oxford University Press, 1995

Sinatra, Nancy, *Frank Sinatra: My Father*, London: Hodder and Stoughton, 1985

Summers, Anthony, and Robyn Swan, *Sinatra: The Life*, New York: Doubleday, 2005

Taraborelli, J. Randy, *Sinatra: The Man Behind the Myth*, London: Sidgwick and Jackson, 2015

Zehme, Bill, *The Way You Wear Your Hat: Frank Sinatra and the Lost Art of Livin'*, New York: William Morrow and Co., 1997

'The blue-eyed ray' was how one close associate described the famously intense Sinatra stare, which could be employed in rage or for romance. On the set of *The Lady in Cement*, 1968

SELECT DISCOGRAPHY

Classic recordings

THE CAPITOL YEARS

Since his death – and particularly in the year of the centenary of his birth, 2015 – there are any number of celebratory collections in the marketplace. There are remastered and repackaged versions of Sinatra's best-known recordings as well as a wealth of previously rare or unavailable material, but the essence of why Sinatra matters can be found in the series of albums originally recorded for Capitol Records between 1953 and 1960, the best of which are supreme examples of an artist at his peak. They include:

Swing Easy
Capitol Records, 1953; producer: Voyle Gilmore; arranger: Nelson Riddle; 10-inch LP
'Just One of Those Things', 'I'm Gonna Sit Right Down and Write Myself a Letter', 'Sunday', 'Wrap Your Troubles in Dreams', 'Taking a Chance on Love', 'Jeepers Creepers', 'Get Happy', 'All of Me'

Songs for Young Lovers
Capitol Records, 1954; producer: Voyle Gilmore; arranger: Nelson Riddle; 10-inch LP
'My Funny Valentine', 'The Girl Next Door', 'A Foggy Day', 'Like Someone in Love', 'I Get a Kick Out of You', 'Little Girl Blue', 'They Can't Take That Away from Me', 'Violets for Your Furs'

In the Wee Small Hours
Capitol Records, 1955; producer: Voyle Gilmore; arranger: Nelson Riddle
'In the Wee Small Hours of the Morning', 'Mood Indigo', 'Glad to Be Unhappy', 'I Get Along Without You Very Well', 'Deep in a Dream', 'I

See Your Face Before Me', 'Can't We Be Friends?', 'When Your Lover Has Gone', 'What Is This Thing Called Love?', 'Last Night When We Were Young', 'I'll Be Around', 'Ill Wind', 'It Never Entered My Mind', 'Dancing on the Ceiling', 'I'll Never Be the Same', 'This Love of Mine'

Songs for Swinging Lovers

Capitol Records, 1956; producer: Voyle Gilmore; arranger: Nelson Riddle
'You Make Me Feel So Young', 'It Happened in Monterey', 'You're Getting to Be a Habit with Me', 'You Brought a New Kind of Love to Me', 'Too Marvelous For Words', 'Old Devil Moon', 'Pennies from Heaven', 'Love Is Here to Stay', 'I've Got You Under My Skin', 'I Thought About You', 'We'll Be Together Again', 'Makin' Whoopee', 'Swingin' Down the Lane', 'Anything Goes', 'How About You?'

Close to You

Capitol Records, 1957; producer: Voyle Gilmore; arranger: Nelson Riddle
'Close To You', 'P.S. I Love You', 'Love Locked Out', 'Everything Happens to Me', 'It's Easy to Remember', 'Don't Like Goodbyes', 'With Every Breath I Take', 'Blame It on My Youth', 'It Could Happen to You', 'I've Had My Moments', 'I Couldn't Sleep a Wink Last Night', 'The End of a Love Affair'

A Swingin' Affair

Capitol Records, 1957; producer: Voyle Gilmore; arranger: Nelson Riddle
'Night and Day', 'I Wish I Were in Love Again', 'No One Ever Tells You', 'I Got Plenty o' Nuttin'', 'I Guess I'll Have to Change My Plans', 'Nice Work If You Can Get It', 'Stars Fell on Alabama', 'I Won't Dance', 'The Lonesome Road', 'At Long Last Love', 'You'd Be So Nice to Come Home to', 'I Got It Bad and That Ain't Good', 'From This Moment On', 'If I Had You', 'Oh, Look at Me Now'

Where Are You?

Capitol Records, 1958; producer: Dave Cavanaugh; arranger: Gordon Jenkins
'Where Are You?', 'The Night We Called It a Day', 'I Cover the Waterfront',

'Maybe You'll Be There', 'Laura', 'Lonely Town', 'Autumn Leaves', 'I'm a Fool to Want You', 'I Think of You', 'Where Is the One?', 'There's No You, Baby', 'Baby, Won't You Please Come Home?'

Come Fly with Me
Capitol Records, 1958; producer: Voyle Gilmore; arranger: Billy May
'Come Fly with Me', 'Around the World', 'Isle of Capri', 'Moonlight in Vermont', 'Autumn in New York', 'On the Road to Mandalay', 'Let's Get Away from It All', 'April in Paris', 'London by Night', 'Brazil', 'Blue Hawaii', 'It's Nice to Go Trav'ling'

Frank Sinatra Sings for Only the Lonely
Capitol Records, 1958; producer: Dave Cavanaugh; arranger: Nelson Riddle
'Only the Lonely', 'Angel Eyes', 'What's New', 'It's a Lonesome Old Town', 'Willow Weep for Me', 'Goodbye', 'Blues in the Night', 'Guess I'll Hang My Tears Out to Dry', 'Ebb Tide', 'Spring Is Here', 'Gone with the Wind', 'One for My Baby (And One More for the Road)'

Come Dance with Me!
Capitol Records, 1959; producer: Dave Cavanaugh; arranger: Billy May
'Come Dance with Me', 'Something's Gotta Give', 'Just in Time', 'Dancing in the Dark', 'Too Close for Comfort', 'I Could Have Danced All Night', 'Saturday Night', 'Day In, Day Out', 'Cheek to Cheek', 'Baubles, Bangles and Beads', 'The Song Is You', 'The Last Dance'

No One Cares
Capitol Records, 1959; producer: Dave Cavanaugh; arranger: Gordon Jenkins
'When No One Cares', 'A Cottage for Sale', 'Stormy Weather', 'Where Do You Go?', 'I Don't Stand a Ghost of a Chance with You', 'Here's That Rainy Day', 'I Can't Get Started', 'Why Try to Change Me Now?', 'Just Friends', 'I'll Never Smile Again', 'None But the Lonely Heart'

Nice 'n' Easy

Capitol Records, 1960; producer: Dave Cavanaugh; arranger: Nelson Riddle

'Nice 'n' Easy', 'That Old Feeling', 'How Deep Is the Ocean?', 'I've Got a Crush on You', 'You Go to My Head', 'Fools Rush In', 'Nevertheless', 'She's Funny That Way', 'Try a Little Tenderness', 'Embraceable You', 'Mam'selle', 'Dream'

Sinatra's Swingin' Session

Capitol Records, 1960; producer: Dave Cavanaugh; arranger: Nelson Riddle

'When You're Smilin'', 'Blue Moon', 'S'posin'', 'It All Depends on You', 'It's Only a Paper Moon', 'My Blue Heaven', 'Should I?', 'September in the Rain', 'Always', 'I Can't Believe That You're in Love with Me', 'I Concentrate on You', 'You Do Something to Me'

Come Swing with Me!

Capitol Records, 1961; producer: Dave Cavanaugh; arranger: Billy May

'Day by Day', 'Sentimental Journey', 'Almost Like Being in Love', 'Five Minutes More', 'American Beauty Rose', 'Yes Indeed!', 'On the Sunny Side of the Street', 'Don't take Your Love from Me', 'That Old Black Magic', 'Lover', 'Paper Doll', I've Heard That Song Before'

THE REPRISE YEARS

Sinatra claimed that some of his last work for Capitol lacked the spark that it might have had because of the discontent he was feeling with his label. It is hard to see any noticeable lack of quality in his late releases for Capitol, even though the final few were contractually obligated albums. Sinatra decided that the only way to achieve complete artistic and financial control of his output was to set up his own independent record company. In December 1960 he officially announced the establishment of Reprise Records. The new label, with the motto 'To play and play again', would offer total artistic freedom to any artist who signed with it, and Sinatra was soon joined by Dean Martin and Sammy Davis Jr. Such legendary jazz artists as Ben Webster, Duke Ellington (who both recorded and produced for the label) and Count Basie joined the roster as well as more established pop singers (Sinatra was apparently keen to sign Andy Williams). The label would also release a number of successful comedy albums.

For Sinatra it was an opportunity to expand his sound and experiment with a number of different arrangers and bands. His first release for Reprise was *Ring-a-Ding-Ding!* in 1961. The title came from one of his personal nonsense phrases that he deployed in various situations and was turned into an anthem by Sammy Cahn and Jimmy Van Heusen. Attempting to distance himself deliberately from the classic Sinatra–Riddle sound of the Capitol years he chose a new arranger, Johnny Mandel. It was both a critical and commercial success and rapidly achieved gold status.

Many of Sinatra's Reprise albums were good, perhaps even great, and suffer only in comparison to his incomparable Capitol collections. Some of the best include:

Sinatra Swings
Reprise Records, 1962; producer: Neal Hefti; arranger: Billy May

Sinatra and Strings
Reprise Records, 1962; producer Neal Hefti; arranger: Don Costa

All Alone
Reprise Records, 1962; producer: Neal Hefti; arranger: Gordon Jenkins

Sinatra and Basie
Reprise Records, 1963; producer: Neal Hefti; arranger: Neal Hefti

It Might As Well Be Swing
Reprise Records, 1964; producer: Sonny Burke; arranger: Quincy Jones

Sinatra at the Sands
Reprise Records, 1966; producer Sonny Burke; arranger/conductor: Quincy Jones

Francis Albert Sinatra and Antônio Carlos Jobim
Reprise Records, 1967; producer: Sonny Burke; arranger: Claus Ogerman

For some commentators his collaboration with Jobim was perhaps the last truly great moment of his recording career. Sinatra's output by the late 1960s was deliberately geared towards achieving chart success, often attempting to cover contemporary songs and employing pop producers. His judgement became increasingly suspect, and there were several low points. Perhaps the most controversial of these, aside from the final, execrable *Duets* albums, was 1980's *Trilogy: The Past, the Present, the Future*, a horribly misconceived three-disc concept album. Its final disc, subtitled *Reflections on the Future in Three Tenses*, explores ideas about world peace and space travel as well as more personal musings and despite being a collaboration with Gordon Jenkins is virtually impossible to listen to. Personal tastes being what they are, however, there are people who apparently – sincerely – also claim that it is Sinatra's finest hour.

You should choose your own Sinatra. For me it is the Saloon Singer whose finest hours were captured at Capitol with Nelson Riddle and Dave Cavanaugh.

INDEX OF COCKTAIL RECIPES BY CHIEF INGREDIENT

Abricotine

Chasen's Banana Punch *116*

Benedictine

After Dinner Special *128*

Vesuvius *129*

Bourbon

Algonquin Cocktail *51*

Benny Goodman's Admiral
  Cocktail *53*

Bob Hope's Rye Lemonade *52*

Manhattan *47*

Old Fashioned *48*

Ward 8 *50*

Whiskey Sour *49*

Whiskey Sour in the Rough *51*

Brandy

El Morocco *134*

Sidecar *75*

Stinger *104*

Vesuvius *129*

Campari

Americano *92*

Cachaça

Caipirinha *87*

Copacabana Cocktail *136*

Champagne

Bellini *167*

Black Velvet *137*

Champagne Cocktail *139*

Death in the Afternoon *101*

Lee Miller's Frobisher *139*

Mimosa *138*

Cointreau

After Dinner Special *128*

Sidecar *75*

Cognac

Prairie Oyster *105*

Gin

Corpse Reviver *103*

Dry Martini *66*

Gibson (1) *71*

Gibson (2) *72*

Layaway *70*

Negroni *89*

Ramos Gin Fizz *100*

South Side *115*

Stork Club Cocktail *132*

Stork Club Cooler *132*

The Vesper *69*

Rum
Bath Cure *118*
Blue Hawaii *84*
Bossa Nova *88*
Cuba Libre *84*
Daiquiri *81*
Floridita Special *82*
Julius Special *131*
Mai Tai *80*
Mojito *83*
Zombie *102*

Sherry
Sherry Flip *118*

Tequila
Margarita *86*
Matador *123*

Vodka
Atomic Cocktail *174*
Bloody Mary *101*
Chasen's Banana Punch *116*
Chi Chi Cocktail *125*
Flame of Love Martini *69*
Salty Dog *161*
The Vesper *69*
Vodka Gimlet *56*
Vodkatini *72*

Whiskey and Scotch
Blood and Sand *122*
Boilermaker *108*
Red Devil *105*
Scotch Rocks *153*

Non-alcoholic
Roy Rogers *172*

INDEX OF WATERING HOLES

New York
21 Club *114*
Copacabana *135*
El Morocco *133*
Jilly's *106*
P.J. Clarke's *74*
Stork Club *129*
Toots Shor's *54*

California
Hollywood:
Chasen's *115*
Ciro's *125*
Villa Capri *90*

Palm Springs:
Chi Chi *124*

San Francisco:
El Matador *119*

Chicago
Pump Room *117*

Las Vegas
The Sands *173*

ACKNOWLEDGEMENTS

Picture credits: pp. 12, 25, 31, 39, 98, 126, 178, 180 Terry O'Neill/ Iconic Images/Getty Images; p. 16 M. Garrett/Archive Photos/Getty Images; p. 32 Bob Willoughby/Premium Archive/Getty Images; p. 40 Express/Hulton Archive/Getty Images; pp. 46, 58 John Dominis/The LIFE Premium Collection/Getty Images; p. 54 Nat Fein/Premium Archive/Getty Images; p. 60 Keystone/Hulton Archive/Getty Images; p. 78 Hulton Archive/Getty Images; p. 94 J. Wilds/Hulton Archive/ Getty Images; pp. 112, 163 Silver Screen Collection/Moviepix/Getty Images; p. 140 Jack Albin/Archive Photos/Getty Images; p. 148 Ron Galella/Ron Galella Collection/Getty Images; p. 155 Popperfoto/ Getty Images; p. 176 Martin Mills/Hulton Archive/Getty Images